Australian Historical Romance

Emily's Baby

LENA WEST

Gymea Publishing

Published by Gymea Publishing

Copyright © 2017 Lena West and Gymea Publishing.

All rights reserved.

No parts of this work may be copied without the author's permission.

https://www.facebook.com/LenaWestAuthor/

www.lenawestauthor.com

ISBN-13: 978-0-6482671-4-0

Lena West

Disclaimer

This story is a work of fiction.

Names, characters, places and incidents are the product of the author's imagination and are used fictitiously. Any resemblance to events, locales or actual persons, living or dead, is entirely coincidental.

Some actual locations may be referenced in passing.

Table of Contents

Disclaimer iii

Table of Contents iv

Dedication viii

1 1

2 13

3 17

4 31

5 39

6 49

7 .... **59**

8 71

9 83

10 89

11	99
12	**107**
13	117
14	**123**
15	**135**
16	**147**
17	**157**
18	**165**
Epilogue	**177**
Here is Your Preview of Home is the Heart	182
About the Author	196
Books by Lena West	198
Connect with Lena!	202

EMILY'S BABY

Dedication

This book is dedicated to my three wonderful brothers, Arthur, Harry and David. Thank you all for encouraging me to fulfil my dream of becoming an author.

EMILY'S BABY

1

He sat on the park bench, an erect, spare figure. An older country man in his Sunday-best navy, pin-striped suit, neatly pressed white shirt and conservative Farmers Federation tie, the whole topped by a broad-brimmed Akubra. The picture of a prosperous farmer down for the Royal Easter Show. He had attended the Show; but the true reason for his presence in the Big Smoke was far removed from pleasure.

Out of sight, his right hand curled around the phial of pills in his pocket. A thermos flask of hot, sweet tea to wash them down stood on the park bench beside him.

The night, mild for mid-April, was perfect.

Perfect for dying.

Distant street lights aided a yellow quarter moon in providing a fitful, shadowy light. Waves thundered and sucked hungrily at the wicked, jagged rocks below the cliffs. Rocks which Hugh Blake fancifully imagined had acquired a taste for blood and despair; and were ravening for more.

His.

If so, tonight they'd be disappointed. His lips curled in a fierce, defiant grimace, distorting his strong, craggy face as he rolled the bottle of pills in his pocket.

Tonight, he'd be dying alright, only not splattered all over the rocks at the foot of the cliff. He'd chosen a tidier option. Kinder too, for those who'd have to deal with the aftermath.

The pills were out of his pocket now and he studied the label, reciting the dosage warning from memory in the darkness. Not that he'd be abiding by those instructions tonight.

He'd waited out the last of the late-night visitors to the park, the last courting couple having departed a good half hour ago. It would be humiliating, as well as defeating his purpose, to be discovered before he'd achieved his goal. So, he'd waited.

Patiently.

Until no-one was left to intervene.

Hugh concentrated his heart and mind on Mary and Andrew whom he'd soon be joining. Five interminable years since he'd lost them, when the Cessna carrying them home to St Denis had crashed with the loss of all on board. Five interminable years of longing to be with them again were almost over. Their family reunion couldn't come soon enough for him.

But he wouldn't be making a hash of his plans tonight through rash, last-minute impatience. A careful man his whole life, he'd bide his time a little longer to be sure of success.

He thought again of his Mary.

His beloved Mary who'd been the only woman in his life.

The only woman he'd ever wanted in his life. His wife through thirty-three years of marriage, was waiting; and he longed to be with her again.

And Andy.

Their baby boy who'd grown to be a man any father would be proud to claim for his own. The son who had brightened every day of his life for almost twenty-two years. The child he and Mary had, for so long, despaired of having, and who had finally been granted to them. Their only chick.

Hugh could feel the triumphant weight of that miraculous infant in his arms still.

Tonight, the three of them would come together again; for all time.

When the doctor he'd come to Sydney to consult confirmed for him that he had cancer and would be dead before the end of the year, he'd dreamed up this scheme. Why should he have to endure an agonising death when he could circumvent fate and die in his own time? On his own terms?

Why should he have to wait a day longer to rejoin his wife and son? He had no other family. No reason to hang on till the bitter, painful end.

Tears of grievous loss; tears of joyous anticipation, blurred his vision. Scudding clouds briefly obscured the moon, casting him into deep shadow on his secluded bench under the trees. Hugh blinked the moisture away, and gasped.

Hand on his runaway heart, he stumbled to his feet; then as suddenly fell back onto the park bench, tremors racking his whole body.

The pill bottle, unopened still and temporarily forgotten, fell to the dusty ground as he stared in fear and joy at the vision confronting him.

They'd come for him, as eagerly impatient as himself!

Hugh attempted to rise, to go to them.

His Mary and his boy who stood before him, pale and luminous in the shifting moonlight. The unexpected pressure of a ghostly hand pushed him back onto the bench, although neither of his two stern-visaged loved ones had moved an inch.

Hugh's heart pounded painfully in his chest.

An icy chill raised the hairs on the back of his neck.

His sudden fear dissolved in the enveloping warmth of a wash of love that flowed over him all at once.

Not this way, Hugh my darling. Tonight is not your time.

Mary's voice, not heard, but felt through every fibre of his being, echoed in Hugh's mind.

This sin will lose you to us for eternity.

Andrew's dire warning vibrating in his bones, Hugh reached despairing hands towards the spirits of his wife and son.

We'll come for you soon. Be strong. Wait for us.

Beatific smiles lit both ghostly faces, beaming a strengthening warmth and joy into Hugh's lonely heart. Fresh, cleansing tears flowed silently from his eyes as his hands dropped to his knees.

Turning from him, his Mary's spirit gazed down the hill towards the road, drawing Hugh's eyes in that same direction.

A slim, blonde girl, her long, straight hair tied back in an untidy tail, trudged wearily into view. Stopping, she peered vacantly about, then taking in her surroundings, uttered a small heart-rending cry and dashed up the path in front of Hugh.

Towards the viewing point above the cliffs.

The jumping off point.

Save them Hugh! For me.

His Mary's urgent words were an order, not a request, and had Hugh instantly rushing to intercept the girl even as Andy spoke the last word.

Help them both Dad. Keep them both safe.

Then the beloved apparitions dissolved into the swirling light fog rising from the water below; leaving only a weeping girl teetering on the edge of the cliff above Sydney's infamous Gap.

And the man rushing to pull her back from the brink.

*****

Dizzy from a day of missed meals; a day of one dreadful shock followed by an even worse one; Emily felt herself sway as if the rocks below were drawing her down; urging her on. Her feet edged forward an inch.

One more step and there'd be no turning back, whether she willed it or not.

And as suddenly as that she knew. She couldn't do it.

Clutching her stomach with protective hands, she forced herself to step back from the edge.

EMILY'S BABY

She was carrying a baby, down there in her still-flat stomach, under her hands.

A precious baby!

For the first time the baby became vividly real to her and a wondrous, loving warmth flooded her heart. She wouldn't be alone any more.

She was going to be a mother! They'd be a family!

Joy was overtaken by fierce determination.

She was going to be a mother who protected her child from all harm.

A mother who nurtured her child.

A mother who loved her child.

A mother who damned her baby's father to the fires of Hell for callously demanding she "... get rid of the bastard before it ruins both our lives."

As if the selfish traitor cared twopence about her! He had no thought for anyone other than himself.

Her eyes closed as if to shut out her pain and shame. Luke had lied to her from the beginning, playing on her loneliness and vulnerability while pretending a love as false as his black heart. She knew him now for the out and out scoundrel he was.

He'd burn in Hell. But she'd live for her baby.

Hers!

Never in her lifetime would that wicked excuse for a man be allowed any part of the precious burden she carried.

Opening her eyes again, Emily saw she still stood precariously balanced on the lip of the jump-off, and hastily shuffled back, bumping into the solid body of a man she hadn't seen approach.

Her thin scream was cut off abruptly when she realised his intent was benign. The unknown man closed his hand around her arm, solicitously drawing her further away from danger.

"Now miss, come away from there. You don't want to be doing that."

His voice was kind. Comforting. Fatherly.

Her mind in turmoil, Emily permitted him to lead her to the bench beneath the trees, well away from the dangerous cliff edge. Although he was a stranger, she sensed no threat. He was just a nice, fatherly bloke who thought he was rescuing her, even though she'd already come to her senses seconds before he intervened.

He fussed gently, offering her his handkerchief to dry the tears streaking her cheeks.

So kind, she thought. This chance met Good Samaritan was so kind.

After the cruelty and shocks of this dreadful day his kindness overturned her heart. Emily burst into a storm of weeping. He carefully turned her into his shoulder, patting her back until her tears slowed to a hiccup and she drew back.

"Here, drink this, Missy. It'll warm you up." He poured tea from his thermos into each of its two cups and pressed the larger one into her hand.

"I'm Hugh Blake," he said, studying her as he spoke.

"I'm sorry for your trouble and would like to help you sort it out. You know, sometimes it's easier to tell the difficult stuff to a stranger, so why don't you use me as a sounding board."

He smiled, inviting her confidences.

Emily sniffed back a stray tear and stared into the gentle, lined face, its blue eyes gazing so openly into hers. She didn't know why, but she instinctively trusted this man. And he was right; talking to a stranger would be easier. Besides, telling him her sordid little tale might help her get her options straight in her own mind at the same time.

Mind made up, she put down her tea to hold her hand out to him.

"I'm Emily Anderson, and I'm the biggest fool on God's green Earth Mr Blake. You can probably guess most of it, but the short version is that I got taken in by a smooth-talking villain who got me drunk one day and seduced me. I thought he loved me. Thought we were going to be married."

She applied the handkerchief again.

Mopping at her cheeks, she mustered up the courage to finish her story.

"Only I thought wrong, didn't I? I ended up pregnant, came to tell him tonight, thinking he'd be happy to do the right thing. Turns out love was a polite euphemism for lust and he's already got a wife and children."

Her voice broke and it took some time to get the next few words out, but her rescuer waited patiently.

"He sh… sh… shoved some money in my hand and t… t… told me to get lost and g… get r… rid of it."

Her lips tightened, recalling what he'd told her when she naively asked what he meant. He'd told her in pretty explicit terms she should find one of those illegal back-street abortionists she'd heard dark whispers about, and pay him to rid her of their baby. Horrified and heart broken, she had run off into the night.

"I felt pretty shocked and scared." A*nd isn't that an understatement,* she thought, bitterness lending an edge to the tone of her soft voice. "I just wandered aimlessly round the streets trying to sort myself out, getting more and more confused and frightened. Until I ended up almost jumping off The Gap."

A shudder ran through her body and nausea roiled in her stomach.

How cliched can you get? she asked herself.

Never in a million years would she have imagined herself in such a situation. As for her Mum and Dad, ... She couldn't imagine what her parents would have said. But that was part of the problem, wasn't it?

Her parents were no longer with her. No longer able to protect her.

"I don't know what I'm going to do now Mr Blake," she said, turning back to her rescuer, "but one thing I'm sure of. The Gap's not the answer. It's a baby inside me and I'm going to do right by it. Somehow."

Her voice, brittle but controlled throughout the bald recitation of facts, broke on the last word and she began sobbing again, quietly and hopelessly.

EMILY'S BABY

It was 1956, and family provided the only help a young, unwed mother could hope for if she wanted to keep her baby.

Emily had no family. No means of supporting herself if she kept her baby. No-one to save her from being forced to give her baby up for adoption.

"Now, now Missy. Emily. It's not the end of the world. People have babies every day. Dry those tears and let's see how I can help. There's bound to be something I can do, even if it's only seeing you to your home."

"You're very kind, Mr Blake, but I don't have a home any longer. My parents died in an accident back before Christmas. I live in a student hostel on the other side of the city; and I'm way past my curfew. I'll be in big trouble with Matron when I get back."

She sniffed back another bout of tears. The broken curfew was yet one more thing added to her ton of grief, insignificant though it was.

"It's not your problem, Mr Blake," she said, straightening her shoulders. "None of it is. In a few days when I've had time to get my head around it all, I'll work something out."

A brave attempt at a smile stretched Emily's trembling lips into a pitiful grimace, wrenching at Hugh's heart.

Bearing in mind his recent divine command to help this girl and her child, Hugh decided to stick to her like a burr in a fleece until he figured out the best kind of help to offer. He'd been given a mission to carry out before he succumbed to the cancer eating away at his gut. There and then, he vowed to succeed in it.

With this in mind, he overrode Emily's protests and took her back with him to his hotel; a short walk away as opposed to the long taxi ride to the suburb where she lived. Once there, he installed her in a room of her own, phoned the matron of her hostel with a story of old family friends visiting the Big Smoke, and extracted a promise from Emily to have breakfast with him in the morning.

Then, he assured her, after a good night's sleep, they'd put their heads together and come up with a fine solution to her problems. Too exhausted to put up more than a token protest, Emily acquiesced.

Hugh Blake's gentle care felt almost like having her beloved father back again.

EMILY'S BABY

2

When the maid knocked on her door next morning with Hugh's note inviting her to join him, Emily was already up and dressed, waiting for the summons, since they'd omitted to designate either meeting time or place. Bracing herself to face her rescuer in the harsh light of day, she set off for the foyer.

Breakfast was to be at the cafe down the road where they could eat on the wide harbourside veranda out of earshot of inquisitive hotel employees. Beyond bland comments on the beauty of the harbour spread out before them, and the glorious autumn weather, neither had much to say until they were sitting in front of heaped plates of bacon, eggs and toast with a huge pot of scalding tea to wash the lot down. Emily's stomach rolled at the smell of the bacon, but she managed a small serving of eggs and toast.

"Mr Blake."

Getting her second wind, Emily was determined to have her say first. Determined to show her rescuer she wasn't always the weak, helpless creature she had been the evening before.

Shudders shook her slender frame yet again at the thought of just how close she'd come to total oblivion.

"Mr Blake, first of all let me thank you for coming to my rescue last night. I appreciate your help more than I can possibly say. But you know, comfortable as my bed at the hotel was, you really should have put me in a taxi and sent me back to the hostel. I have no right to let you waste your valuable time on my trivial problems."

"Trivial problems! Good God girl! Don't you let me hear you calling a baby a trivial anything. You hear me! A baby can be a lot of things, Emily, but never trivial."

Emily recoiled from his harsh tone, much relieved when he relaxed and continued mildly.

"I considered sending you off. For about ten seconds at least."

A wry smile flashed, then he was all seriousness again.

"Let me tell you my story, Missy, then you'll be better able to understand why I'm so fired up to help you. I wasn't up at The Gap last night to admire the stars, you know."

Emily's mouth dropped open and her complexion paled at least two shades as she intuited his meaning.

Hugh pulled out the pill bottle he'd retrieved from under the seat the previous evening, setting it on the table between them.

He stared at it in brooding silence while he composed his thoughts.

"I intended to take my own life. With those." A nod towards the innocuous brown chemist's bottle.

It was one thing to suspect, and an entirely other thing to hear her suspicions so baldly stated. At Emily's sucked in gasp and horrified expression, he looked up, face a pained grimace.

"Let me tell you my story," he repeated.

Before his tale was told, tears streamed down Emily's cheeks and her two hands had reached across the table to clasp Hugh's firmly between them.

A few stray drops of moisture tracked down his own cheeks.

"So, you see my dear, when a man is told by visitors from the other side that he must do a thing, he better do it to the best of his ability, or risk eternal damnation. No more bravado from you now, girl. Your job is to help me fulfil my destiny."

Fierce brown eyes stared from beneath grizzled brows as he dared Emily to defy him, softening to tenderness when she merely nodded and sniffed back her tears.

If she was to keep her baby in spite of all the odds stacked against her, she needed help. Maybe this kind, fatherly chap had been sent by the Fates to provide that help. He seemed to think he had at any rate.

The least she could do was listen to what he had to offer. She owed her baby that much.

The discussion of ways and means lasted through two more pots of tea and an early lunch before they reached a strenuously argued consensus.

The final clincher had been Hugh's heartfelt plea to Emily to be the daughter he'd never had and ease his dying with her companionship.

"Have pity, Emily. If you refuse, you're forcing me to face what's coming alone, and last night proves I'm not strong enough for that. You and the little one will give me courage. Please don't deny me, Lass."

Although they'd be like father and daughter, he stipulated, they would go through a paper marriage to give Emily respectability in the community, and her baby an honourable name. Since the cancer eating away his life would see Hugh dead before Christmas, and most of that time she'd be bound up in her pregnancy, Emily felt it was a very small portion of her life to dedicate to the man who was promising her security and the means to bring up her child.

Freedom from the threat of being forced to give it up for adoption, and the stigma of its being labelled a bastard was worth a lot more to her than Hugh was asking.

He was right. Her innocent baby deserved the best, and if it gave him pleasure to provide for the two of them without hurting anyone else, she would accept gratefully; even though everything within her recoiled from making such a mercenary bargain.

Even so, it would be no easy ride, Emily knew. She would require a great deal of intestinal fortitude to stand against the gossip mongers of Hugh's world; but for the sake of her baby she would take on far more than that.

3

Outside the train window Emily saw kangaroos leaping away from the lines. Occasionally an emu or two paced the train until they were left in its wake. And then there were the sheep. Hundreds of merinos, their white coats red-brown with dust, as far as her eyes could see.

On the surface she was thrilled, burying her disquiet as deep down as she could.

How will I fit in? she wondered. *I've never been further west than the Blue Mountains. I'm entering a foreign land, here in the Outback.*

It would be a poor return for Hugh's kindness to subject him to her cowardly misgivings. She pinned her brightest smile on her face; and asked another question about this wide, brown land where the Earth met the sky with not the tiniest of hills to mar the perfection of its flat, distant horizon.

All day Emily chattered brightly to Hugh, enjoying the stories he told of the places they passed through. Stories of exploration, gold and bushrangers. Stories of the aboriginal peoples and the European settlers who had displaced them, claiming the land for their own. Exciting stories, sad stories and several downright hilarious stories. For the next several months at least this wide, dry, dun coloured country would be her home. Its stark emptiness was more than a little daunting.

It was such a huge contrast to the wet, green coast where the profusion of little towns and great cities overflowed with people.

People, she realised during the afternoon, were the one thing she wasn't seeing out the window of the train relentlessly clattering and chugging its way west. Yet it was people, the people waiting at the end of the ride, who were tying her insides in knots, resulting in a nausea worse than any morning sickness she'd so far endured.

During the preceding days Hugh Blake had given her his staunch support while she resigned from college, with considerable regret for the teaching career lost to her because of her untimely pregnancy.

Yet another thing Luke stole from me, she thought bitterly.

Hugh had then taken her shopping for clothes more suited to life on a sheep station than those she already possessed. He'd showered her with gifts galore, even when she laughed, protesting that she didn't need a single thing more. She accepted them gracefully, only when she realised how much fun Hugh was having spoiling her as if she really were the daughter he'd longed for, yet never had.

Later he'd visited his lawyer and his bank manager, taking steps to ensure the financial security for herself and her baby which he had promised her. When all that was done, he'd taken her to the courthouse and given her his name, so neither she nor her child would ever have to hang their heads in shame.

Now he was taking her home. To his home, *Emu Downs Station*, out across the plains beyond The Great Divide near the town of St Denis.

A town which Emily had discovered was included only on the most detailed of maps.

"It's only a small place compared to the cities you're used to, Em," Hugh had said, "but you'll find it possesses all the necessary amenities, and anything you can't buy in our shops can be ordered from Sydney and sent up on the train."

Unable to imagine what else she could possibly need after Hugh's amazing generosity, Emily looked forward to exploring St Denis with mixed feelings.

Just as she looked forward with mixed feeling to meeting the other members of Hugh's surrogate family who shared *Emu Downs* with him.

Mrs Duffy, his elderly housekeeper, and her husband Charles, a stockman at *Emu Downs*. And the station manager, Ryan Farrelly, whom Hugh had told her he regarded almost as a second son.

There were other men working on the property too, but they lived in the bunkhouse and took care of their own needs. She didn't think she'd be having much to do with them. They weren't family like Ryan Farrelly and the Duffys.

For the sake of the baby, Hugh, as she was learning to call her new husband, had coached her in her new role of happy bride, although he'd hastened to reiterate, it was to be in name only.

"There'll be no casting aspersions on our baby's parentage," he ordained.

"If we both play our parts well enough," he assured her, "everyone will accept me as the baby's legitimate father."

Although the fact he considered it necessary to warn her confirmed Emily's suspicions that his friends would look askance at her.

And at her marriage. But, hopefully not at her child.

Emily gazed at the strong, work-toughened man of the land sitting bolt upright in the seat opposite her. He had a good face, she thought. The lines fanning out from the corners of his eyes and the deep creases bracketing his mouth indicated a strong character leavened with humour; all of which she had already discovered to be the truth. His face told her of a well-lived life. The brown, sun-dried leathery skin told her of a long, full life lived in the open air, and she smiled at the pale band across the top of his brow left by the Akubra which protected his salt and pepper hair from sun and weather. Looking at him today, it was hard to imagine he was a dying man, he appeared so solid and enduring.

Then the guard walked through the carriage, coming to a halt at Hugh's side.

"Five minutes to *Emu Downs* siding," he warned them.

Five minutes until the charade begins!

Fear clutched at Emily's stomach and drove the colour from her cheeks. Seeing it, Hugh reached across to take her hands and give them a little shake.

"Buck up Emily. I'll be right beside you, you know. They'll undoubtedly be a bit standoffish at first, but only until they get to know you. Then they'll take you to their hearts as I have. They're good people, Girl. Even if they don't approve at first, they'll all be polite to you for my sake. You'll see."

Emily blinked back the cowardly tears threatening to spill over and worked up a bright smile for Hugh. She smoothed down the lovely circular tartan skirt, bought from the David Jones Department Store, drawing courage from its cheerful red checks held stiffly away from her body with its voluminous net petticoat. Worn with a collarless cream silk blouse and black velveteen peplum jacket that showed off her still trim waist, she was confident she looked her best. She straightened her neat little felt hat, tugged at her gloves, and, head up, flashed a wan smile at her protector.

After all Hugh had done for her; all he'd given her; the least she could do was look happy and not shame him.

Holding that thought, she picked up her brand new, beautifully soft leather handbag, gathered together her magazines, and steeled herself to face the hazards of her new life.

*****

Careful of the ever-present danger of bushfire, Ryan Farrelly ground the butt of his hand-rolled cigarette into the dirt with the toe of his scuffed work-boot. Moodily he kicked at a stone, wondering what the boss's new wife would be like. Wondering how much she'd change things on the station.

He didn't like change. Didn't want it. There'd been too much change in his life and it had rarely boded well for him. Memories of being left a penniless orphan when his father was killed in a sawmilling accident flashed through his mind. He'd stayed in school until the system had cut him loose, then drifted from one job to another until he'd fetched up on *Emu Downs*.

Hugh Blake had taken him in hand, and into his home, training him to become a station manager. Hugh held his heart; and his loyalty.

The Boss had picked the woman up during his holiday in Sydney, so he guessed she'd be a smart city woman. Most likely full of complaints about the dust and flies and the stink of sheep.

Well, too bad for her. She's snared herself a rich pastoralist and dust, flies and smelly sheep are part of the package.

If she came on all la-di-da playing lady of the manor, he imagined Joan Duffy would soon put her in her place.

As for him, there was a vacant cottage behind the machinery shed that would soon find an occupant if she gave him any grief.

He worked for Hugh; and no toffee-nosed fancy piece out for what she could get was going to change that.

He kicked the stone again, looking down the tracks as he heard the train whistle at the level crossing. A glance at his watch confirmed that for a change it was on time. He straightened his shoulders and tugged his battered, sweat-stained Akubra firmly into place.

It was time to meet the new missus. Ryan mentally rehearsed the polite words Hugh would expect to hear.

*****

"Ryan! Good of you to come yourself."

Hugh, first out the door of the first-class carriage, shook hands and clapped his station manager, who was also his friend, on the arm, not waiting for an answer.

"Give the guard a hand, will you mate. I'll see the wife down safely and be right along. She's got quite a few bits and pieces back there."

As Ryan turned towards the luggage van at the back of the train, where the guard was valiantly dealing with a collection of suitcases and packing boxes, he caught a glimpse of a pretty girl in swirling skirts passing a pair of hat boxes down to Hugh. Long golden hair and long, slender legs almost had him turning back for a better view, but the train was on a tight schedule and the guard needed a hand, so he hurried along to where he was needed.

Surrounded by baggage, Ryan looked round as the train chugged off down the line into the sunset, to see Hugh and the girl who'd caught his eye approaching him.

Who the hell is she?

Where's Hugh's wife?

Sitting in the car like Lady Muck, I suppose, he answered his own question, *while I have the fun of carting her luggage into the shelter-shed. And then I'll still have to come back again with the ute,* Ryan grumbled to himself a bit more. He cast a sour look over the mountain of luggage the woman had brought with her. More than would fit into the Holden, that was for sure.

Is the girl her maid or her daughter? Daughter, he decided, when she linked arms with Hugh, saying something which made him laugh.

No maid would dare to be so familiar with her employer's husband. Ryan straightened his back and stepped forward to do the pretty.

The daughter was an unexpected bonus, he decided, his mood lifting as he got an eyeful of a dimpled smile and brown eyes lit with sparkling tawny highlights. Girls were thin on the ground out here, and one this pretty would draw every young fella from miles around, like bees to a honeypot.

She sure is a pretty little thing.

His heart gave an odd lurch, and he thought smugly that being first on the scene gave him an indisputable head-start on the rest of the pack.

Unless, of course, she had her mind set on winning the heir to one of the rich properties round about. Once he'd have included himself among their number. Now, he wondered again, as he had too many times since the arrival of Hugh's telegram announcing his marriage, what the chances were of the Old Man coming good on his promise to make him, Ryan Farrelly, his heir?

Same as a snowball's in Hell, he reckoned. *A woman smart enough to get her hooks into Hugh Blake won't stand for seeing him leave Emu Downs out of the family. Hell, she might even be young enough to produce an heir of her own.*

Well, Ryan straightened his shoulders as he reached Hugh and the girl, *I've made it this far without anyone handing me a silver spoon. No reason I need one now.* Though it cost him to say goodbye to his dream of farming *Emu Downs* himself one day.

While the men sorted out the luggage Emily had done some looking of her own, silently assessing this rangy, whipcord-muscled young man who was so important to Hugh. For Hugh's sake she wanted to like him, only she was doubtful she would.

She was sadly lacking in both confidence and trust after her experiences with Luke.

She already knew Ryan Farrelly was coming up to his thirtieth birthday, young for his position of station manager; from which she could safely assume he was intelligent, hard-working and competent. He'd have to be to satisfy Hugh. Although generally easy going, she'd noticed her husband expected value for money. A sentiment she found no fault at all with. She intended to meet his expectations herself. Down to the last detail.

As for the rest, Ryan Farrelly certainly looked attractive in a stern, no-compromising way, with eyes grey flecks of stormy sea-water glinting between eyelids perpetually half closed against sun and dust as Hugh's were. At first glance the full sensual mouth appeared at odds with the severity of the rest of his image.

Maybe, she mused, *he has hidden depths.*

Well, time would tell, and anyway, she wasn't at all interested in him personally, was she? At best he'd hopefully be something of a brother figure. At worst, well, she'd only be here a few months. She'd just keep out of his way.

"Got the lot, then? Lord, Ryan, you should have seen the fun we had with this lot at Central Station," Hugh chuckled. "Should have called ahead and told you to bring Charlie and the ute as well as the Holden. Sorry I didn't think of it. Leave those boxes a moment, Son and come say hello to the missus. Emily, I'd like you to meet my right-hand man, Ryan Farrelly. Ryan, meet my wife, Emily."

His wife!

EMILY'S BABY

That pretty little girl is Hugh's wife!

Ryan stood there gaping like a stunned mullet. Recovering his wits, he shut his mouth with a snap and slowly stuck out his right hand.

"Welcome to *Emu Downs*, Mrs Blake."

"Good afternoon, Mr Farrelly."

His tersely rasped greeting had been a split second too slow for true politeness and earned him a very cool, slightly amused reply in an English accented voice.

A Pom into the bargain! Bloody Hell!

Ryan ducked his head to hide his thoughts till he could get his face in shape again.

What the hell did Hugh think he was doing, marrying a girl young enough to be his daughter; if not his granddaughter?

No need to speculate on her motives though. Rich older man meets pretty young gold-digger. The story sprang, fully formed, into Ryan's mind.

One down, two to go.

Emily held on to her pleasant little smile like grim death.

Ryan Farrelly hadn't been quick enough to hide his contempt from her. A metaphorical slap in the face, it hurt; even though she'd been expecting it. Emily sighed.

He won't be the only one to look down his nose at me either, she was willing to bet, *so I'd better grow myself a hide as thick as an elephant's, or I'll never survive.*

If not for Hugh pointing out interesting sights, the short drive from the siding to the sprawling, single-story wooden homestead with its elegant encircling veranda would have taken place in silence as Ryan fumed over Hugh's getting himself caught in such an obvious honey-trap, and Emily ignored him, busy marshalling her courage to meet the Duffys.

A meeting which was pretty much a repeat of the one with Ryan Farrelly.

Mrs Duffy, a thin, desiccated woman bundled into an out-sized pinafore over her tidy skirt and blouse, looked as if she'd been sucking lemons. If Emily hadn't been smarting from the sting of the older woman's disapproval, she might have laughed.

Instead she felt more like crying.

Until she heard a hissed "Behave yourself, Woman!" from Mr Duffy as she followed Hugh down the hallway to her room.

Maybe she had one ally among the staff after all. Perking up, she plastered a fresh smile onto her face, refreshed her lipstick and prepared to make the best of things.

*****

"We all eat together, Emily. No standing on ceremony here, we're all one big happy family," Hugh said, holding Emily's chair for her a little later.

"It makes more sense than everyone eating in different places round the house. Less work for Joan, too."

"Of course, that can easily be changed if you'd prefer it otherwise, Mrs Blake." Joan Duffy, nose in the air, still looked pinched and disapproving.

"Why would I want to change such a sensible, democratic arrangement, Mrs Duffy? And please, call me Emily. I'm not used to formality."

It took a considerable effort, but Emily held the other woman's eyes and even managed a tiny, polite smile while doing so.

"That goes for all of you," she added, broadening her smile, and her gaze, to include the other members of the party. "I'd like it if you'd all called me Emily."

She let her gaze rove around the table, from one stranger's face to the next. Her smile brightened at Hugh's beaming grin and conspiratorial wink, in spite of the quite audible sniff from Mrs Duffy.

"And I'm Charlie, Emily."

Charles Duffy, lanky, grey haired and as cheerful as his wife was acidulous, jumped in to fill the hiatus following Emily's invitation.

"I like what you said, about us being democratic and all that. The wife's Joan," he added, nudging his wife's elbow.

"Yes. Please call me Joan, Mrs Blake." Charlie nudged her again. "I mean Emily."

The woman unbent enough to accompany her words with a near facsimile of a smile without any further prompting from her husband.

Emily reckoned she owed Charlie Duffy, and she wouldn't forget it. Her bright face still intact, her eyes settled expectantly on the fifth person present at the dinner table.

"Call me Ryan, Emily."

Something in the way Ryan Farrelly stared at her left Emily breathless and bewildered.

His tone and cynical stare had implied more than a simple invitation to use his Christian name, only it was a message she didn't understand.

Flustered, she averted her gaze and lifted a forkful of feather-light pastry.

"Please, don't let this lovely meal get cold. Joan, you must have sixth sense, choosing steak and kidney pie. It's one of my favourite dishes, and your pastry is even lighter than my mother used to make."

"You'd go a long way before you found a better cook than my Joan," Charlie loyally chimed in. "I can tell from the pretty way you speak that you're from the Old Country, Emily."

"That's right, Charlie. We came out after the war, as Ten Pound Poms. It was the best decision my parents could have made. We all loved Australia right from the first."

To Emily's relief, the men soon began a desultory conversation about farm matters, leaving her to listen and learn while she tucked into her meal. When Joan stood to clear away the empty plates and bring out the trifle she'd made for dessert, Emily jumped up to help.

"Sit down Emily. I can manage well enough on my own. I'm used to it," Joan admonished stiffly.

"I know you can, Joan. But you've got help now. You know, many hands and all that. Besides, I'm dying to get a look at your kitchen."

When Emily helped clear away at the end of the meal, staying in the kitchen to help with the washing up, Joan muttered under her breath about people getting under her feet.

"I'll try not to get under your feet, Joan," Emily interjected, letting her know she'd heard every word, as she supposed she'd been meant to.

It was also intended to tell the older woman she wouldn't be backing down. She was the new mistress in this house, and the sooner Joan Duffy accepted it, the better. If she didn't take a stand immediately, she'd never earn the older woman's respect; and she refused to exist as a down-trodden mouse, despised in her own home. Not even for the few short months she expected to live here. In spite of their rocky start, Emily hoped she and Joan could learn to work amicably together.

"I'll wash, you dry," she said, seizing the initiative. "That way I can watch and see where everything belongs. My mother always said the best place for two women to get acquainted was over a sinkful of dirty dishes."

Slipping off her rings and watch, Emily began running hot water into the sink. Silently, Joan picked up a tea towel and set the draining rack ready.

4

The next morning, Emily rolled out of bed with a groan, summoned by the alarm clock.

If she was going to make any headway with Joan Duffy she couldn't afford to lie around in bed until the queasiness abated. She thanked the Lord her morning sickness was mild enough not to have her retching her heart out and throwing up every morning.

She took a moment to admire all over again the pretty room adjoining the master bedroom. It had once been the nursery, but Mary had redecorated it as a guest room when Andrew Blake had outgrown it.

Now it was hers, chosen for her by Hugh because the connecting door gave them the public appearance of living together as husband and wife, while each maintained their privacy.

Dressing quickly, she made her way to the kitchen in time to help serve breakfast to the men before they headed outside to do whatever it was men needed to do on a farm.

Then she helped Joan clean up and hang out the laundry that, while they ate, had chugged away in the state-of-the-art washing machine, the like of which she had never seen before outside of an appliance showroom.

She'd worried a little that a farm, way out in the bush, wouldn't have much in the way of modern amenities, but Hugh had laughed her fears away.

"We've got a generator to provide our own electricity, and I made life as easy as I could for Mary and Joan by installing the latest labour-saving machines money can buy," he'd proudly informed her. "It's alright, Emily. You won't have to rough it pioneer style. Not on *Emu Downs*."

She believed him now. She'd seen nothing but the best of everything since she'd arrived the afternoon before.

Twin lines of washing dancing jauntily in the breeze, Emily stuck like glue to the housekeeper, helping to sweep and dust and generally make herself useful till morning smoko.

"I've enjoyed my morning, Joan," she said.

A prevarication, but only a small one. She'd detected a slight softening in the older woman's attitude, enough to encourage her to continue her efforts at winning her over.

"Hugh wants to show me around the yards before lunch, and I thought, if you're not too busy, you might show me over the house this afternoon?"

Emily smiled brightly at Joan's terse nod.

"We need to work out a proper routine, don't we, to share the work efficiently. Will you give some thought to which jobs I can do for you, or help you with, Joan? We can talk it over later."

Emily didn't expect to be waited on and had been at pains to make that quite clear to Joan Duffy. But neither did she intend to tolerate insolence from her, and she'd subtly made that quite clear too.

They might never be friends, although she did hope they could learn to deal amicably with each other. Life at *Emu Downs* would be rather miserable for her if they didn't.

Hugh had almost completed his tour when Ryan and Charlie rattled into the yard in the ute, a pair of kelpies jumping down to frisk around the men's legs.

"They don't usually come in for lunch," Hugh explained. "Only if they're working close to the house like today. Hey Charlie," He waved the stockman over, leaving Ryan to load fencing wire into the back of the ute on his own.

"You're always complaining about having to look after the chooks. How do you feel about handing them over to Emily?"

"Sounds good to me, mate. Never did like chooks, unless they're on the menu," he grinned at Emily. "Only tolerate 'em for their eggs. Clucking and carrying on all day."

"Well, I do like them Charlie. Especially when there are new little chickens." Emily thought the large brown hens looked friendly, and she could do with all the friends she could get on *Emu Downs*, even if they were only hens.

"I was thinking, Hugh. If Charlie doesn't mind, I would enjoy helping in the gardens. My Dad was a gardener, and he taught me quite a lot. The vegetable gardens are beaut, but the flower beds are a bit rundown. I would feel I was contributing something if you'd let me help out."

"No problem Lass, as long as the boss here has no objections."

"None at all. I'm glad to see you making a niche for yourself Emily. We've got plenty of water and all the space you can use. Mary was the gardener, and after she died, except for the vegetables, it all got overgrown and neglected, until it ended up the eyesore it is now. If you're sure it won't be too much, it would make me happy to see the gardens restored. Mary loved her flowers," Hugh added wistfully.

He looked around at the overgrown beds, a sad, far-away look in his eyes. With a little shudder, he returned to his companions, and the conversation.

"I'd sure like to see all the flowers back again. Any help you need with heavy digging, just ask Charlie or Ryan."

"Then that's a deal, Hugh."

Emily linked her arm through her husband's and leaned companionably against his shoulder, smiling mistily up at him.

I'll have the gardens blooming in spring, she vowed silently. It was the least she could do to repay all Hugh had done for her.

"Charlie can go on growing the vegetables, and I will grow flowers where you can see them from your chair on the veranda."

How touching!

Ryan sneered to himself, spotting them as he rounded the corner of the house on his way to wash up for lunch.

The girl can certainly be given top marks for effort.

The thought of Emily wasting her youth and beauty on an old man turned his stomach. The fact he liked and respected Hugh Blake only made it worse, somehow. When she turned her head to watch his approach, he felt a stirring in his loins. An unwelcome stirring that further soured his mood.

Irrationally, he blamed Emily.

What is she up to? he thought savagely. *Isn't her husband enough for her? Does she want to have every man on the place panting after her?*

Scorn curled his lip as he eyed her through narrow slits hidden beneath the broad brim of his hat.

Sure, she's a pretty, sexy package, but I've got her measure. She needn't think Ryan Farrelly is going to be a lapdog like Hugh. Or Charlie, he added scornfully. *Look at the silly old bugger hanging on her every word.*

Emily glanced back over her shoulder as she went to wash her hands for lunch and caught Ryan staring at her again in a way that made her feel distinctly uncomfortable. Something dark and enigmatic in his expression made her think of danger, but surely she was being ridiculous. Hugh trusted the man. She shivered, and quickly turned her eyes back to the front, still feeling his boring into her back.

"Ryan, there you are. Come on, let's not keep lunch waiting." Hugh led the way up to the wide, shady, fly-screened veranda where Joan was wheeling out a heavily laden trolley to the table where the men could eat in their work clothes and boots without messing up her clean floors inside.

"By the way, Emily's going to set the gardens to rights, so I'd appreciate it if you can let her have Charlie for the heavy digging sometime in the next day or so."

"Christ, Hugh! We're up to our eyeballs in work and you're taking Charlie away to dig gardens! If he's going to become a gardener, I'll need another stockman to take his place."

Ryan felt his annoyance was fully justified. He and Charlie had been working overtime trying to keep the place going while Hugh swanned off to Sydney for a couple of months holiday at one of the busiest times of the year. He'd already been home almost a full day, but he didn't seem too eager to get back on his horse and out on the run where he was needed.

If he wants to hang around the homestead and play house with his child bride, why can't he dig the damn gardens?

"I've been giving that some consideration, Ryan. Charlie and Joan are planning to retire in the next year or two and I'm not getting any younger. You may as well get someone now and have him learning the ropes. Is there anyone you know of who might suit?"

Conversation over lunch was centred on possible candidates for the new man, leaving Emily to sit back and listen. She understood Hugh's need to find someone quickly and was content to leave it to him to decide on the right time to share news of his tragic state of health with the others.

She sympathised entirely with his wish to defer that confidence as long as possible.

He didn't want to be seen as a feeble old man on his death bed any sooner than he had to. No man would.

Lunch was nearly over when Hugh introduced a new topic.

"Joan, do you think you could handle a buffet dinner Friday next week? Emily will help, won't you Em?"

He'd already discussed his plans with her, so, although her stomach clenched in apprehension at the thought of the party, she gave an affirmative answer. It was something they had both decided was not only necessary, but better done sooner than later if she was to make friends among their neighbours.

"I'd like to have a few friends and neighbours over to meet Emily. I thought about thirty people."

"Certainly I can cope, Hugh." Joan bridled at the tacit implication she mightn't. "Just you leave it to me."

Smiling, Hugh agreed to do exactly that.

"I'll ring around tonight and let everyone know, then. Quicker than sending out written invitations."

*****

Emily and Joan soon came to terms with sharing the housework, and when Emily flattered Joan by asking for cooking lessons, she saw the older woman's face adorned with a genuine smile for the first time since she'd arrived.

Tactfully, she let Joan take the lead in planning the party, simply following directions in polishing the best silver, bringing out the good glasses and china and helping to give the floors and furniture an extra buffing up.

She was beginning to take a housewifely pride in Hugh Blake's lovely home.

EMILY'S BABY

Beginning to feel it was her home too.

5

Nervously, Emily studied her reflection in the cheval glass standing in the corner of her bedroom. The street-length pale pink satin dress with its figure hugging off-the-shoulder bodice requiring a strapless bra, swirled around her knees, held wide by a flurry of petticoats. Matching satin covered shoes with a higher heel than she usually wore made her legs look long and elegant, her ankles delicately slim.

On her wedding day in Sydney she'd worn the same dress with the prettiest little floral hat and matching bolero, but for tonight's party both had been set aside. She'd chosen a pair of pearl studded hair clips to match her Granny Anderson's pearl necklace; her something old. Her something new had been a pearl engagement ring given to her by Hugh. On hearing about the wedding, the receptionist at the hotel had loaned her a prayer book covered in soft, blue leather, to carry in place of flowers. Something both borrowed and blue.

She applied her make-up with a light hand, and, surveying herself critically, decided she'd do.

Too late if she didn't.

EMILY'S BABY

A car rattling across the cattle grid announced the arrival of the first of Hugh's guests.

By the time Dr and Mrs Partridge reached the veranda, Emily was standing by Hugh's side where she remained for the next half hour, being introduced to everyone as they arrived. Some guests she'd already met on a trip into St Denis with Joan, but most were new faces.

On the whole, they were less censorious, at least to her face, than she'd feared. One notable exception was the Dalgleish family - husband, wife and daughter, a raven-haired beauty in her mid-twenties. All three stared down their noses at her and sailed past with the barest of civilities.

"Don't judge the rest of us by their example, will you Emily."

"Oh." Emily turned to the latest arrivals, smiling widely in welcome. "Susan, I'm so glad to see you."

While in town, Joan had introduced her to Susan Brandon, a young bride of her own age, and the two of them had hit it off immediately. Emily was sure she and Susan were destined to become best friends during her stay at *Emu Downs*.

"Vivienne Dalgleish and her parents think they're a cut above the rest of us," Susan whispered behind her hand. "Mostly we ignore them and let them think what they like. Congratulations Mr Blake," she added in her normal speaking voice.

Susan leaned forward to kiss, first Emily, then Hugh on the cheek. Turning back to Emily, she introduced her family.

"Emily, I'd like you to meet my husband, Andrew, and my parents, Ron and Barbara Elliot from *Wallaroo Station*."

Susan's family were as friendly and unaffected as Susan herself, chasing away the uncomfortable chill the Dalgleishes had left in their wake.

Shortly after, Emily and Hugh left their post at the top of the steps and joined their guests inside where Joan was handing round canapes and Charlie manned the make-shift bar in the corner. Bing Crosby crooned softly from the stereogram, the music almost drowned out by the chatter of friends who met infrequently and had a lot of catching up to do.

Opting for a glass of Coca-Cola, Emily made her way round the room, spending a few minutes chatting with each group of women, the men having drifted out onto the veranda where they could smoke and indulge in masculine conversation. Vivienne Dalgleish was noticeable by her absence, and a quick glance through the open French doors showed her in animated flirtation with a group of men, not all of whom were single.

When Joan brought in the platters of cold meats and salads, the dynamic shifted, the men once more deigning to mingle with their womenfolk, helping themselves to the buffet meal. Between the main course and dessert, Hugh tapped his spoon against his glass. When he had everyone's attention, he made a pretty little speech thanking his friends for coming and hoping they would all look upon his new wife as yet another friend and an asset to the district. He concluded with a toast to his bride, Emily.

"Wife! Huh. Believe me, Hugh Blake will live to regret being such a fool as to marry that designing young female."

In carrying tones, Mrs Dalgleish confided her opinion to her crony, Mrs Smythe, as conversation resumed.

EMILY'S BABY

Was it merely a coincidence, Emily wondered, that she was standing no more than a yard or two away at the time, where she couldn't help overhearing?

Suddenly she was tired of turning the other cheek. Tired of placating narrow-minded bigots who should have been spending their time minding their own affairs instead of hers.

Snapping her plate down almost hard enough to break it, she stepped forward with a tight social smile.

"Why, Mrs Dalgleish, how good of you to be so concerned for my husband's welfare. I'm so glad to know Hugh can rely on your support, but he won't need it. I'm going to take such good care of him he'll never have the slightest cause to regret marrying me."

While the noise of distant conversations echoed in the air around them, a pool of silence surrounded the two women as those in earshot listened with bated breath. The pink in Emily's cheeks was due to more than her carefully applied rouge.

"Here we are ladies," Joan Duffy hurriedly elbowed her way through the crowd with her tray.

"Who'd like dessert? Mrs Dalgleish? It's pavlova, your old favourite."

"Oh yes, Mrs Dalgleish, you must have some. Joan's a champion pavlova maker," Emily urged, grateful to be rescued from the consequences of her own intemperate tongue.

"Let me help, Joan."

She eased the tray of desserts into her own hands, serving Mrs Dalgleish and Mrs Smythe then circulating through the room.

"Nasty old bat. Here, I'll give you a hand."

Susan Brandon began helping Emily fill the now empty tray with dirty glasses and plates to be returned to the kitchen.

"I'm glad you stood up to her Emily. She's always lording it over the rest of us and poking her nose into other people's business."

"Maybe, but I was rude to a guest, Sue. I ought to apologise to her, but I don't think I will. She was far ruder than me first. I think I'll beat a strategic retreat to the kitchen with this lot and give Joan a hand for a bit."

"I'll come with you. There's probably a fresh pot of tea in the kitchen, and I know I'm ready for a cup."

Chatter and laughter died abruptly when the two girls appeared in the doorway to the kitchen, signalling to Emily that she, and probably her social gaffe, had been the topic of conversation.

Gritting her teeth, she deposited her tray on the table, and made a beeline for Joan Duffy, surprising the housekeeper as much as herself by clasping her in a bearhug.

Tears threatened to spill, but she sniffed them back, refusing to show weakness in front of the gaggle of older women. Easing back, she looked Joan in the eye and favoured her with a wobbly smile.

"Thank you for coming to my rescue, Joan. You saved me from making an even bigger exhibition of myself than I already had."

Dropping her hands, she lifted her chin and turned to face the others.

"I apologise if my bad manners made anyone uncomfortable."

"Go on with you, Lass. You've no need to apologise for anything. If anyone should be apologising, it ought to be Mavis Dalgleish. It did my heart good to see you stand up to her. We've all been letting her get away with far too much, in the name of peace and quiet."

Barbara Elliot patted Emily on the shoulder and a chorus of affirmative comments rang in Emily's ears from the rest of the gathering.

"Thank you, Mrs Elliot. All of you." Slightly dazed by their partisanship, Emily gazed about her.

"Joan says you're a good girl and that's good enough for us," Barbara Elliot continued her role of spokeswoman.

"You're a station wife now Emily, just like the rest of us, and that carries responsibilities in this community. It's not too early for you to start taking your proper place as Hugh Blake's wife. There's a C.W.A. meeting next Thursday. Joan will bring you along and I'll second your application for membership."

Stunned, Emily stared open mouthed. The Country Women's Association, an Australia-wide women's organisation formed to improve conditions for women and children, especially in rural districts, wanted *her* for a member! A rosy blush staining her cheeks, Emily drew in a deep breath.

"Mrs Elliot," she gasped. "Oh Mrs Elliot, I'll be there. My mother would be so proud. She always maintained, the day she was accepted as a C.W.A. member was the day she truly felt like a real Australian."

"That's settled then. Why don't you grab yourself a cup of tea and sit on the veranda with Sue for a few minutes? You'll be doing me a favour if you can get her off her feet for a bit."

"I will, but first I think I should give Joan a hand with the washing up."

"All taken care off, Emily." Joan waved her hand around to indicate the roomful of women. "I've got more help than I can poke a stick at. As the guest of honour, you're excused this time. Shoo."

She thrust a cup of tea into Emily's hand and urged her out the door.

*****

"Come on Em. Let's go catch you up on the local gossip."

Susan Brandon linked her arm through Emily's and led her to a pair of chairs further down the back veranda.

It felt so good to have a friend of her own age. Emily hadn't realised how much she'd missed having a girlfriend until she found one. She listened idly to Sue rattling on while she sipped at her tea, content to have a few minutes of time-out from her duties as hostess.

"Sue, why did your mother say I'd be doing her a favour if I got you to sit for a bit? Are you unwell?"

The question had been circling in Emily's mind and just popped out when Sue's chatter ran down for a minute.

"Oh," Sue giggled. "It's not a secret, although not too many know yet. Andrew and I are expecting a baby in December."

"How wonderful! You must be so excited."

Emily only just managed not to blurt out the news of her own pregnancy. She supposed she owed it to Joan Duffy to tell her first, but Sue would be next on her list of confidantes. It would be wonderful to compare notes with her. One more thing they had in common.

"It is, but Em, let's move to the front veranda. I can hear dance music, and I want to dance. Besides, I'm not giving Vivienne Dalgleish a chance to get her hooks in Andrew again. He went out with her before me, you know. She threw him over because he wasn't rich enough for her. Even so, she was pretty narky when he took up with me soon after, and tried to come between us. Real dog in the manger stuff. She's never happy unless she's got a man in tow. Preferably more than one."

And Vivienne had one now; very firmly in tow.

But why Emily should feel sick to her stomach with a nasty sense of betrayal at the sight of Vivienne dancing cheek to cheek with Ryan Farrelly, she was at a loss to understand. Turning her back on the couple who appeared totally engrossed with each other, she went to slip her hand under Hugh's arm, standing patiently at his side till Bert Wallace finished the yarn he was spinning. Hugh laid his other hand over hers and winked at her.

"There you are, Em. I wondered where you'd got to. Like to dance?"

*****

After the last of their guests had departed and the household had retired for the night, Emily knocked on the connecting door to Hugh's room.

She entered without waiting for a reply.

Her husband looked up from his struggle with his cuff-links, mutely holding his wrists out to Emily. Obliging him with a helping hand, she said what she'd come to say.

"I won't keep you more than a moment, Hugh. I just wanted to thank you for a lovely party. I had fun, and your friends are really nice people, just as you said they were. Also," she hesitated, stiffening her resolution to go on, "I need to apologise to you. I was unforgivably rude to Mrs Dalgleish. I'm not sorry for that, she deserved it, but I shamed you in front of your friends, and that I am sorry for."

"Now Em," Hugh hugged her briefly. "You could never shame me. Certainly not over Mavis Dalgleish. It made me proud to see you stand up for yourself. The gossip hasn't been easy on you, and it's not going to stop any time soon. Best thing to do is ignore it. Most people don't mean any harm by it, you know."

"I know. You're a very nice man Hugh Blake. I'm glad I came to *Emu Downs* with you."

On that felicitous note Emily retreated to her own side of the connecting door and closed it softly behind her.

So why did she drift into sleep wishing Ryan had danced with her instead of Vivienne?

EMILY'S BABY

6

A new farmhand, a cocky young chap by the name of Jimmy Plunkett, arrived on Monday, easing Ryan's and Charlie's workload. He was quartered in the bunkhouse with the other men, but he seemed to spend an inordinate amount of time hanging round the homestead trying to ingratiate himself with Hugh and the women.

"Calling me 'Grandma'!" Joan spluttered. "He's too cheeky by half. Too full of himself, that young Plunkett."

Emily was inclined to agree with her. His sly smiles and sneaky winks made her uncomfortable in an entirely different way to when Ryan Farrelly looked at her with his measuring glances. Jimmy Plunkett's presence upset the order of things around the homestead, and not in a good way. However, another man was needed, and he'd done nothing to actually justify her making a complaint, so she simply made a point of keeping out of his way.

Two days of much-needed soaking rain had kept Emily indoors except for quick dashes across the backyard to feed the hens and collect the eggs.

Finally, the sun showed itself again, so, dressed in work pants and serviceable shirt and jacket, Emily pulled on rubber boots and attacked the weeds and grass choking the front garden, grateful when Charlie joined her for two afternoons in a row to help with the heaviest of the work.

There were still shrubs struggling to survive in the abandoned garden, and she discovered dormant bulbs in the soil around them. They provided an excellent backbone to be fleshed out by the packets of seeds and punnets of seedlings for winter flowering annuals she'd bought on her last trip to town.

All in all, Emily felt her life was settling down. It was such a good feeling after the doubts and worries of recent weeks.

Returning to the garden on Wednesday morning, the ground ready at last for her precious seedlings, she was humming *Blue Moon* a recent hit by the young American performer, Elvis Presley, who was taking the world by storm, as she collected her tools from the shed.

When Jimmy swaggered in she nodded curtly, trying to ignore his leering smirk, and continued with what she was doing, eager to make her escape from his unwelcome presence.

Next minute he'd crept up behind her. Swinging her round in his arms, he kissed her. A hard, wet, scarily unpleasant kiss. Before she got her wits back, he kissed her again, pawing roughly at her shirt, and making her head spin and her insides freeze in fear.

For all of half a dozen heartbeats, until her instinct for self-preservation kicked in.

She was frightened, but she refused to be cowed.

Jimmy shouldn't be touching her like this. Shouldn't be touching her *at all*. It was wrong, and she wouldn't tolerate it. Wrenching her mouth from his, she swung her hand and slapped him as hard as she could across his too handsome face, leaving a stinging red welt the shape of her hand on his cheek.

"Come off it Emmy! Don't make out ye've never been kissed before," he hissed, furious at being repulsed.

"Ol' Blake may think ye're all sweet innocence, but I know better. Yer landed yerself a cushy billet here on *Emu Downs*, but when yer get tired of bein' an old man's plaything, just yer let me know. I know 'ow ta give a Sheila a good time. Meanwhile, I'll give yer somethin' ta be goin' on with."

Jimmy grabbed at her again, but Emily, thoroughly riled and horribly afraid, was having none of it.

Recalling a piece of practical advice from her father when she was getting ready to go out on her first date, she kneed Jimmy in the groin. Hard. Then, while he was doubled over holding his privates, shoved him away from her.

Gasping in pain, Jimmy fell to the floor, curled into a protective ball.

"Yer bitch!" he gasped. "What'd yer want ta do that for?"

Afraid of retaliation, Emily grabbed up the garden fork she'd dropped and stood back from him, holding it at the ready.

Expecting an easy victory, Jimmy now found himself eye to tines with a dangerous weapon wielded by a girl who seemed blood sister to the Furies. He lay very still. When the battle-haze faded from Emily's eyes, he edged back and raised himself onto his elbows. He was about to speak but Emily got in first.

"You may not think much of me for marrying a man old enough to be my father, Jimmy Plunkett," she hissed, furious still, yet icily sure of herself now she'd got the better of him, "but that doesn't give you the right to treat me like a slut. Does it?"

She thrust the fork towards his throat, emphasising her question. He was forced to raise his hands to protect himself.

"Does it?" she demanded again, her voice rising in volume. She thrust the fork at his face again.

"Na. Na it don't," he muttered.

"Then you keep your filthy hands off me in future, or I'll make you sorry, you worthless heap of dung. I'm Hugh Blake's wife; and I won't be treated like dirt by you or anybody else. Remember that! Now get out of my sight."

Emily, fork still held at the offensive, stepped back to allow him to get up from the floor.

Cursing a blue streak, Jimmy scrambled to his feet and backed off to a safe distance.

"What in blue blazes is going on?"

Ryan Farrelly, tight-lipped and bristling with rage, stood, hands on hips in the open doorway, taking in the scene.

"Nut'un, Farrelly. I were just gettin' the fence strainer like yer said." Jimmy grabbed the strainer off the bench and slunk past Ryan out the door, beating a hasty retreat, unaware his face still bore the imprint of Emily's hand.

Cold grey eyes tracking his exit, Ryan let him go. For now.

He'd keep.

He turned those same cold, grey eyes upon Emily, who had dropped the fork as soon as Jimmy cleared the door. Pale and shivery with shock, she trembled, fighting back tears now the crisis was over.

"Did that bastard hurt you, Emily?"

Despite his words, his icy, somehow accusing, tone scared her all over again, although in quite a different way, reducing Emily to a stutter when she answered him.

"I... I'm o..okay, R..Ryan. He s..scared me a bit, but I d..dealt with him."

She sure did, Ryan thought, reluctantly admiring her resourcefulness.

He'd arrived in time to witness the conclusion of their encounter. What he had seen and heard had made him madder than a Mallee bull. Right now, though, suffering the aftermath, he reckoned Emily would do better with a bracing dose of practicality than with being molly-coddled.

"You're not okay. Look at you, you're shaking like a leaf. Here sit down before you fall down."

Voice rough at the edges, he impatiently dragged an oil drum over and urged Emily to sit.

Outwardly solicitous, inside Ryan was seething, his momentary admiration deliberately set aside. He'd known from the first the girl was going to be nothing but trouble, and this little episode confirmed that opinion. He supposed she'd been leading that idiot, Plunkett, on and got more than she'd bargained for. His temper surged anew, thinking of the two of them together.

Feeling moisture gathering in the corner of her eye, Emily fumbled for her handkerchief.

And now she's crying for sympathy, Ryan raged. *Well, she won't be getting any from me!*

He'd better get to the bottom of things and then he supposed he'd have to waste more time reading the riot act to Plunkett.

"Tell me what was going on," he ordered. "When I arrived, it looked like you were fighting him off. Looked like you'd dealt with him pretty effectively too."

The sneaking admiration he'd felt earlier returned, just a little, before impatience edged it out.

Taking a deep breath, he summoned a return of the sternness he'd initially shown. Hands planted on hips, he stood over Emily, and got back to the real issue.

"But I still want to know what happened."

Emily wiped shaking hands over tear-dampened cheeks and eyed Ryan warily.

The set expression on his face made it clear he wasn't going anywhere until he got the whole story out of her, so she surrendered to the inevitable and poured out her pitiful tale.

"Ryan, I don't want to make trouble," she concluded, "but Jimmy scared me."

It was worse than he'd expected, if she was telling the truth, and in spite of his initial suspicions, he was beginning to think she was.

Ryan studied the down-bent head with its smooth cap of straight, tied-back golden tresses and had to force himself to resist the urge to take the distressed girl in his arms and comfort her.

Comfort her; and more.

Which would make him every bit as bad as the nasty piece of work she'd just fought off. Disgusted with himself he slapped his dusty hat against his thigh and ploughed his fingers through his hair.

"I thought at the time, Hugh made a mistake hiring Plunkett," he finally told her. "Leave it to me, Emily. I'll see to it he doesn't bother you again."

An order she was only too happy to obey.

This time the impatience causing his clipped tones was directed entirely at himself.

"You know something Ryan?" Still shaken, Emily spoke her thoughts out loud.

"I was prepared for all the flak I'd have to face, marrying an older man. I believed as soon as people got to know me properly, they'd begin to think better of me. I still believe that; but nothing prepared me for the sort of abuse I just copped from Jimmy Plunkett. And you know something else, Ryan?" She lifted her head, meeting him eye-to-eye.

"Even knowing that, I'd make the same choice every time. Hugh Blake is the nicest, kindest, decentest man I know. I married him for love, not his money. I would have married him if he hadn't had a bean. Although I'll admit the money is a useful bonus."

It was true, Emily thought. Every word she'd spoken was the truth.

She had married for love.

Love of her baby, which she was very much afraid she'd have been forced to give up for adoption without Hugh's timely intervention. No-one would have given her respectable employment. Without a family to support her, she simply wouldn't have been able to afford to bring up a baby on her own, no matter how much she loved and wanted it. Only she didn't feel it necessary to add that qualification to her statement. No-one else knew about the baby yet, and on Hugh's advice she was keeping quiet about it as long as possible.

Emily's declaration hit Ryan as hard as her hand had hit Plunkett's cheek.

Was it aimed at him? He wondered if she had read his lust for her in his attitude and was using this opportunity to warn him off.

It made him sick to the stomach to be lumped in with that lousy excuse for a man, Jimmy Plunkett; and sicker still to know he deserved to be.

Sister Mary Loyola, back in his convent school days, had drummed it into her students that the thought was as evil in God's eyes as the deed, and now his Catholic conscience was giving him hell.

Aside from that fact, as if it wasn't bad enough, his hunger for Emily constituted a grievous disloyalty towards Hugh.

It was time to take all his frustrated longings elsewhere, though damned if he knew where.

He gave himself a mental shake and looked the distressed woman in the eye, hoping she read his more honourable intentions in his.

The intention to treat her like his little sister from now on being chief among them.

"Come on, Em," he urged. "I'll see you back to the kitchen and Joan will make you a cup of tea to soothe your nerves."

Ryan put a hand under her elbow to help her up, making an impatient noise when she shook him off.

Dismally, Emily thought she could sure do with a nice hot cup of tea, only she was afraid Joan might blame her for the incident and she'd be right back to where she'd started with Joan Duffy. At the moment she couldn't scrape up the energy to face another battle for acceptance.

"Thanks Ryan, but no thanks. I came outside to do a job and that lout isn't going to stop me. That'd be letting him win, don't you see?"

Emily gathered up her scattered tools and, head high, marched off to the front garden. If some of her seeds were watered in with tears, that was nobody's business but her own.

*****

Vivienne Dalgliesh rang that evening, demanding to speak to Ryan.

As if it were the answer to his prayers, Ryan jumped to accept her invitation to a little party she was having for a few friends. Vivienne was an attractive, available woman whose charms would hopefully insulate him against Emily's.

His boss's wife had begun taking up too much of his attention.

It had to stop.

7

Under Barbara Elliot's sponsorship, Emily had been accorded a warm reception by the C.W.A. ladies, most of whom were delighted to welcome the new wife of one of the district's principal landowners into their midst.

Those who hadn't attended the *Emu Downs* party, but who'd heard the gossip doing the rounds, were pleasantly surprised to find neither the vacuous ninny Irene Smythe had described, nor Mavis Dalgleishes' brazen hussy. Instead, they discovered her to be her a shy, modest young woman, perfectly willing to defer to her elders. Although, to a woman, they still had unanswered questions about Hugh Blake's hasty marriage.

Since the ladies were busily knitting and sewing to stock their stall at the upcoming hospital fete, Emily asked Joan to take her to buy wool and fine white lawn to make baby clothes. The fete, combined with Sue's expected baby gave her a legitimate excuse to be seen constructing tiny garments. No longer was she forced to hide preparations for her own child away in her room. It surprised her how long she'd managed to keep her secret, but it shouldn't have.

With Autumn well advanced, she was wearing bulky, warm clothes which effectively hid her changing shape from view.

Another bonus, since the party Ryan had been invited to, there'd been neither sight nor sound of the Dalgleish women, who, she discovered from listening to the ladies' chatter, had gone to Melbourne on a shopping holiday. Emily hoped they planned a long, long stay in the southern capital.

Something about Ryan Farrelly spending time with Vivienne Dalgleish set her teeth on edge. Was it because she simply didn't like the woman, or was it more to do with the uncomfortably possessive feelings she had recently developed towards Ryan? The vague disloyalty towards Hugh which these feeling engendered within her caused Emily to shy away from probing her subconscious for an answer. Instead, she contented herself with counting her many blessings.

On her last trip to town she had taken a driving test, Charlie, her instructor, having declared her ready, and now she had a brand-new driver's licence. Hugh, especially, had been pleased with her.

"Everyone needs to be able to drive in the bush," he declared, beaming with pride. "Well done Em. Most people learn when they're kids, bumping round the paddocks in old farm utes. You're fast becoming a true countrywoman."

Now she could go to town, or to call on Susan without depending on someone else to take her. She revelled in her independence. Hugh had offered to buy her a car of her own, an offer she had gently refused. He had given her so much, she felt guilty just thinking of adding a car to the tally when she and Joan were happy sharing the Holden.

Her garden was coming along nicely, too, and a new man had been hired to replace Jimmy Plunkett who'd been unceremoniously paid off and given his marching orders.

Mick Jones, pleasant and sober-mannered, was a stocky, hard-working man in his late thirties. Even better, he had a lady friend, Pauline Marsden, whom he planned to marry as soon as the jackaroos' cottage was spruced up a bit to accommodate a woman. A vast improvement on Plunkett, he already fitted in on *Emu Downs* as if he'd been born there. Pauline, born and bred on an outback cattle station, had come out from town for a visit and won Joan's seal of approval with less than a quarter of the time and effort it had taken Emily.

Life wasn't all blessings though.

Coming out of remission, Hugh had had a bad spell; Dr Partridge being sent for to make a home visit. The result had been full disclosure of his condition to the members of his household. The shock of it had hit Ryan and Charlie particularly hard, more so since they'd been thinking harsh thoughts about Hugh's skiving off doing his share of the outdoor work.

Joan, who'd seen far more of Hugh in recent weeks and developed suspicions of her own regarding his health, was less surprised, although his fatal diagnosis had still come as a dreadful shock to her.

Alone in her prior knowledge, Emily discovered herself standing as a bulwark between Hugh and the fresh grief of his surrogate family.

He had weathered this attack, but it had weakened him to the point where he could no longer pretend there was nothing wrong with him.

While ill, he'd formed the habit of relying on Emily to fetch and carry and entertain him while he was confined to his bed; not that she minded one iota. It was part of the deal they'd made, and she was pleased to be able to repay his kindness in this small way.

The whole household was striving to adjust to the new state of affairs, and Emily was ashamed and guilt-stricken to find an insidious relief in the way Hugh's ill health now haunted all minds, ousting previous preoccupation with his precipitous marriage. While overjoyed to be relegated to second place on the gossip charts, she could only wish it hadn't come at such a high cost.

*****

June roared in, cold and unfriendly with blustery winds, scudding showers and frost on the open ground. When, finally, a day dawned calm and sunny, it tempted Emily outdoors once again.

Seeking solitude while Hugh rested after lunch, she wandered down towards the creek, passing the yards where Ryan and Charlie, their dogs sitting obediently outside the rails, were working with the horses.

Since the episode with Jimmy Plunkett she felt a special bond with Ryan Farrelly, albeit an entirely one-sided one. He made her feel safe; and something more.

Something she avoided defining. Usually she enjoyed watching him as he put the horses through their paces, but after a week of being housebound by bad weather, she longed for freedom and kept on her way with no more than a cheery wave.

An hour of peace and quiet, enjoying the birdsong and chattering of water rushing and gurgling over the rocky creek bed restored her equilibrium. Turning for home Emily eschewed the path, scrambling up the muddy bank to walk back across the home paddock; a much shorter route which had the added advantage of taking her close to the horse yards where she planned to linger a few minutes, watching the animals being schooled. She refused to countenance the idea it might be watching Ryan, not the horses, which posed the greater attraction.

Over at the yards, the men spun round at the sound of a blood curdling scream that cut off abruptly.

Ryan, stockwhip still in hand, vaulted the rails and hit the ground running. There was only one creature in the Australian bush capable of inspiring the fear behind Emily's scream.

A snake.

But was it a harmless python or grass snake or one of the deadlier serpents? His mind rapidly processed the scene before his eyes, planning ahead even while he sought to avert impending disaster from a distance.

"Freeze! Freeze, Emily! Don't move a muscle!" Ryan shouted.

He was close enough to discern Emily's white-faced terror, before he spotted the long, sinuous, dark body swaying back and forth above the grass, too close to the woman for safety. Slowing his headlong rush to a more cautious approach, Ryan offered Emily a stream of comforting reassurances while drawing the king brown's attention away from the woman and towards himself.

Judging the distance nicely, he flicked the stockwhip. In a blur of speed, the lash sang through the air, landing in a ringing crack that broke the venomous snake's back.

Charlie, slower off the mark, had armed himself with a sharp-bladed, long handled shovel and circled into position to back up Ryan's attack on the deadly snake. In seconds he'd severed its head from its writhing body, reducing it to harmless carrion.

A queer little female moan wiped the triumphant grin from Ryan's lips. Dropping the whip, he sprang forward with an oath, snatching Emily's falling body into his arms, bare inches above the red dirt.

Seeing Emily fall to the ground, Ryan felt his stomach plummet even lower. She couldn't be dead! Not Emily! Not the beautiful girl he loved!

Loved!

He couldn't be in love! Not with Emily, the girl who'd sold her youth and beauty to an old man in exchange for his wealth.

Never in a million years! With his whole being he rejected his moment of epiphany. When he fell in love, it would be with someone worthy of that love.

"Struth, mate. Did that brown bastard sink his fangs in before you got to 'er?" Charlie threw a vicious glance over his shoulder at the dead snake.

His question forced Ryan back to reality, and the unconscious girl in his arms. Not dead, he realised, noting the steady rise and fall of her chest. Even the deadly venom of a brown snake didn't take effect that quickly.

"Dunno Charlie. I'll get her up to the house. Let Joan check her out."

Not hanging round to debate the issue, Ryan strode off across the paddock with Emily, unconscious and deathly pale, cradled tenderly in arms that trembled more from reaction than the weight of their burden.

Charlie, grabbing up the whip and shovel, shot another ferocious glare at the now harmless snake and hurried to catch up with Ryan.

*****

"Where were you bitten? Emily, Goddammit! Tell us where you were bitten."

Groggily, Emily peered up at Ryan, frowning to understand his urgency and the fear so clearly evident in his voice. As she regained her senses she began to remember.

"Oh! The snake," she shuddered.

"Yes! The damned snake!" Ryan shook her impatiently, urging her to focus and answer his question.

"Where did it bite you Emily? Tell us so we can deal with it."

"But it didn't." Emily struggled to sit up, becoming annoyed when Ryan pushed her back onto the cushions of the cane lounger.

"What happened?"

"Let the girl alone, Ryan."

Joan pushed in front of him and took Emily's hand between both of her work-roughened ones.

"You passed out Emily. Can you tell us if that snake bit you? If it did, we need to get you to the hospital as quickly as possible so the doctor can administer the antivenin."

"No. No, I remember now. I surprised the snake sunning itself on a patch of bare ground. I got a shock, meeting it unexpectedly like that, and I screamed. But I knew to keep still, so I did. I thought if I stayed still long enough it would go away, but Ryan was there first. And you, Charlie. Thank you. Thank you both."

Emily smiled mistily at the two men leaning over her. "You were both so brave, killing it like that. But it didn't bite me. I'm alright. Really. I don't know why I fainted. That's not like me. I never faint."

"Well, today you did."

Hugh eased himself onto the seat beside her, patting her arm with tender concern.

"Are you quite sure you're alright, my dear? You were unconscious for a long while. From the time you fainted out in the paddock until Ryan carried you back here. You gave us all a real scare."

"Quite sure, Hugh dear. I never meant to be such a nuisance and I'm quite alright now," she repeated.

To prove it Emily sat up straight, swinging her feet to the floor.

"Well, I'm almost alright," she amended as the sudden movement triggered a wave of nausea that rolled through her stomach and leached from her face what little colour she had regained.

"I'm just a bit unsettled still from the shock. I'll be right as rain in a minute. I'm so sorry to have frightened you all."

"Don't give it a thought, my dear." Hugh steadied her with an arm round her waist. "You just sit still for a bit and let Joan bring you a nice cup of tea. In fact, why don't you bring us all one Joan. I'm sure we could all do with it."

Gratefully, Emily leaned her head against Hugh's shoulder, content for the moment to be taken care of. With Hugh's arm supporting her she felt protected from all harm as she always had in the past when her father had comforted her small hurts.

Sorry!

Ryan almost snorted at the pathetic little apology. *The damned woman scared ten years off my life, collapsing in my arms like that, making me think she'd suffered a fatal snake-bite, and all she has to say is 'Sorry'. And as for all that sweet lovey-dovey nonsense with Hugh just now, the pair of them were enough to turn a man's stomach.*

Especially if the man found himself wanting that particular woman more than was good for him.

But I'm not in love with her, he told himself again. What he felt was lust. Just lust. Never love. That simply wasn't possible.

Ryan turned his back on the pretty scene he found so offensive, deciding to leave them to it and get back to the horses. Too late. Joan was on her way back with the tea trolley and Hugh was ordering him and Charlie to fetch chairs so Emily didn't have to move from where she was. Shaking off his black mood, Ryan sauntered around the veranda to comply with his instructions.

EMILY'S BABY

"You know Emily," Joan said as she handed the younger woman a steaming cup, "I've been thinking, and I believe there may be another reason you fainted. Besides the snake, I mean."

She smiled knowingly, woman to woman, and paid close attention to the self-conscious glance Emily exchanged with Hugh.

"Nothing escapes you, does it, Joan. I knew we couldn't keep our little secret from you for long. It's time to come clean, Em."

Hugh gave Emily's hand a gentle squeeze and kissed her on the cheek. Turning back to the interested gazes of the others, he grinned proudly as he made his announcement.

"Emily and I are expecting a baby. Sometime soon after New Year," he added, anticipating Joan's next question.

The date he quoted was almost a month later than the true time the baby was due, but Hugh had persuaded Emily to accede to the mild deception to make his claim of paternity more convincing. Dr Partridge, the only one privy to the truth, was sworn by friendship and patient confidentiality to support their story.

"We were only waiting till we were sure before sharing the news."

"I knew it!" Joan could hardly contain her delight. "I told Charlie just the other day I thought there was some good news in the offing."

"She sure did. You can't pull the wool over my Joanie's eyes," Charlie affirmed with a chuckle.

During the flurry of comments and congratulations it passed unnoticed that Ryan's good wishes had been a trifle forced.

Neither did anyone think it significant when he took advantage of the earliest opportunity to escape.

"If you've finished that tea, Charlie, we'd better get back out to the horse paddock and finish up the job," Ryan ordered when Joan urged Emily to lie down and rest for a while, till she was completely over her shock.

He felt sick and angry all over again and fisted his hands in his pockets to keep them from getting him in trouble.

How can a girl as young and lovely as Emily stand an old man like Hugh touching her intimately? A sick old man, he reminded himself. He might not be in love with her, but he was certainly attracted to her. Too much so for his own good.

I reckon this baby puts paid to the last of my hopes Hugh will keep his promise regarding the future of the farm.

No-one had ever handed Ryan Farrelly a free chance at success in the past, and it looked as if that was the way it would continue. He was on his own; just like always.

Lips clamped tightly, he jammed his hat on his head and stalked off, not waiting to see if Charlie was following.

*****

That evening it was Ryan who phoned Vivienne, who'd recently returned from Melbourne, with an invitation to dinner and dancing at the club in town.

EMILY'S BABY

8

Joan Duffy wasted no time spreading the news round her circle of friends, so Emily wasn't the least bit surprised to see Susan Brandon and her mother, Barbara Elliot, drive up to the front gate one afternoon.

"Wonderful news, Emily," Susan called out before she was out of the car. She rushed up the steps to fling her arms around her friend, her mother following more sedately. "Are you excited? I bet you are. I reckon our babies will grow up the best of mates, don't you Emily?"

Baby talk occupied all four women until they were sitting around the kitchen table with their first cups of tea in hand, when Barbara broached a more serious topic.

"I hear Hugh's not been too good," she said. "Bad enough to haul Dr Partridge all the way out here. I hope he's alright now."

Joan and Emily shared a moment of silent communication, the happy smiles disappearing from both their faces. With a sigh, Emily placed her cup carefully back on its saucer and lifted her eyes to meet Barbara's shrewd gaze.

"No, he's not. He's got cancer. That's what his trip to Sydney was for, Barbara. The specialist told him he won't live to see another Christmas."

"Excuse me." A sob caught in Emily's throat, and with a muttered apology she ran out onto the veranda, handkerchief to her eyes. Susan ran after her, folding her friend into her arms and murmuring soothing nothings into her ears till Emily had herself in hand again.

"Sorry Sue. I didn't mean to turn on the waterworks, but these days I seem to cry at the drop of a hat."

"It's the baby," Susan assured her confidently. "I'm just the same. Up in the air one minute and down in the dumps the next. Not that I'm saying you don't have good reason to get teary. Don't give it a thought Em." More soberly, Susan held Emily by the shoulders, looking her firmly in the eye.

"I'm really sorry about Hugh, and that's the truth. He's a lovely man and a good friend to our family. Even though you haven't been together for very long, he's your husband, so it's much worse for you, Emily. Whenever you need a friend, be sure you can count on me."

This time it was Emily doing the hugging and Susan's eyes which teared up.

"Thanks Sue. I have a feeling I'm going to need all my friends before this is over. Hugh and I have talked about it, and we've decided to make the most of the time he's got left, not brood over the unfairness of it all. Come on, let's go back and finish that cuppa, then I'll take you along to look at the nursery things Charlie hauled out of storage for me." She laughed, recalling the scene.

"He spent an hour dusting it all off this morning. Ryan was spitting chips about him being late getting out to finish checking the fences, but Hugh told him to back off."

"That reminds me, Em. I've been hearing a bit of gossip about your Ryan getting himself involved with Vivienne Dalgleish. Is it true?"

"Seems to be. They've been out together a few times now, and I heard Ryan on the phone last night inviting her to the club again tonight."

"Shame. A decent bloke like Ryan getting mixed up with someone like Vivienne. He could do a lot better for himself. Oh well, he's not the first to have his head turned by a woman like her; all show and no substance."

Arrived back at the tea table, the girls let the subject drop, but Emily sat down hard, appalled to realise she could now name the sick feeling she experienced every time she thought of Ryan and Vivienne together.

It was called jealousy; the emotion Shakespeare had dubbed the 'green-eyed monster', and she had no right to be feeling it. No right at all.

Later, when she was alone again, she retreated to the privacy of her bedroom to examine her feelings.

It took a bit of rationalisation, but she eventually concluded her jealousy didn't mean anything inappropriate. Ryan had twice come to her rescue and she had developed a sense of possession towards him, as she would an older brother, in spite of knowing he didn't approve of her.

She simply had to become more independent.

Simply had to guard against relying too heavily on him.

*****

"I suppose now the news is out, we'll be inundated with visitors, curious to see for themselves," Ryan grumbled, when Joan reported on Barbara's and Susan's visit during dinner.

"Possibly, Ryan," Joan snapped back in a tart voice. "However, I think our real friends are more likely to be sympathetic than vulgarly curious. Don't you Charlie?" She looked to her husband for corroboration.

"Reckon so," Charlie agreed amiably. "You're pretty well liked hereabouts, Hugh." He turned to his boss, simple honesty and liking lighting his homely features. "Got a heap of friends who'll all want to see you while you're still up to it."

Charlie's prediction proved correct, as over the next few weeks more visitors than usual dropped in on a variety of pretexts from checking out some of the *Emu Downs* rams which were due to go on sale in the spring, to discussing who should be elected as the new representative to the Farmer's Federation now Hugh would be handing in his resignation. Joan and Emily seemed to be forever refilling the biscuit tins, as good manners dictated every visitor be regaled with a cuppa.

On his good days, Hugh sometimes asked Emily to drive him into town, or to friends on another property. One such trip was to keep an appointment with his solicitor, Harry Emden, which Emily found mildly surprising as she thought he'd settled his affairs while in Sydney.

"Just a couple of loose ends I missed, Em. Nothing to worry about," he'd said.

"Thought I'd take the opportunity to sort it out today, then we'll have a nice lunch at the pub. The *Southern Cross* does a nice roast."

As they entered the dining room of the *Southern Cross*, the best hotel in town, the Dalgleish family followed close on their heels. To Emily's consternation, Hugh immediately invited them to join himself and Emily. Thinking her dislike of Vivienne was based mainly on Susan's prejudiced opinion, Emily strove to find some common ground with the other young woman. It was heavy going, but she persevered, determined to make amends for her gaffe at Hugh's party. Besides, she reasoned, if Ryan was serious in his pursuit of Vivienne, then she was likely to find herself in the other woman's company from time to time. It made sense to establish a pleasant relationship.

Or try to. On closer acquaintance she still didn't like any of the Dalgleishes very much.

"Sorry to inflict that lot on you Em," Hugh said after making the irreproachable excuse of a doctor's appointment to leave as soon as the meal was finished. "The thing is, Brad phoned the other day, suggesting we ought to get together soon. While I'm still able, is what he meant. A whole evening of Mavis playing lady of the manor was a bit more than I felt up for, so I said I'd get back to him."

A dry chuckle let Emily know her antipathy to the Dalgleishes was shared.

"When I saw them come into the dining room, I jumped at the chance to dispense with my social obligation over a quick lunch instead of a long, boring evening."

Emily squeezed his hand.

"Good thinking, Hugh. Though I suppose we'll have to put out the welcome mat for Vivienne if Ryan wants to invite her to the house."

"If that happens," he winked, "I think I'll probably be too poorly for guests. In which case I'll need you keep me company, Em."

And that's what happened a couple of weeks later, when Vivienne roared up to the front door in her bright red sports car and invited herself to dinner before hauling Ryan off for an evening's dancing at the club.

To Emily's amusement, Joan set a fancy table for them on the veranda and retreated to the kitchen with Charlie.

*****

Vivienne came to visit several more times before the end of that long, cold winter. Unfortunately, by then Hugh's excuse of illness was totally genuine. He was keeping to his room more and more, wasting away before their eyes. When he did emerge on his better days, it was merely to lie on a daybed on the veranda for an hour or two. Tiring quickly, and having lost his appetite, he'd recently given up joining the others for meals, preferring to have a tray in his room; although he insisted Emily join the others, claiming it was unhealthy for her and the baby to spend every minute of the day stuck in the sickroom.

Still, Emily spent a lot of time at his side, reading to him, playing a hand or two of cards, or talking quietly. On sunny days she'd coax him onto the veranda where he enjoyed surveying his paddocks. They were looking their best, all green and fresh from winter rain, and brought a bitter-sweet joy to Hugh's heart.

It was promising to be a bumper season. A good time to go, he reckoned.

He'd thought a lot about the events of the night he and Emily had met. With time he'd rationalised away all hint of the supernatural, convincing himself he had dreamed the encounter with Mary and Andrew, although it would have been more comforting if he could have believed he'd actually seen them. Spoken with them.

Even so, if he had it to do over again, he'd still have chosen to give Emily's baby a name. Still have brought her back with him to *Emu Downs*. She was keeping her side of their bargain without complaint, and he had grown to love her as the daughter he'd never had. Sometimes he daydreamed she was Andy's widow, and her baby his grandchild. He found it a particularly comforting fantasy.

Thinking of Emily, he turned his head to watch her knitting a jacket for the baby and smiled to himself. If his plans worked out, she'd have more than a baby to bring her happiness after he was gone. He'd seen how Ryan watched her, a brooding look putting a scowl on his face. It was the look of a man with strong feelings he didn't know what to do with. Hugh smiled again, reviewing the steps he'd taken to give his two favourite people a chance to find happiness together, just to be sure he'd not missed anything important. It was to be hoped Ryan's friendship with Vivienne Dalgleish petered out before the man committed himself to a future he'd later regret.

Turning his eyes outward once again, Hugh looked closer to home, the show of early daffodils nodding their golden heads in the front garden bringing a warmth to his heart. Mary had planted the bulbs, he remembered.

It gave him a pleasant feeling of continuity to see them still blooming long after she was gone. The sight of them made her feel close.

He was as near contentment as it was possible to be with the cancer eating away at him. At least the painkillers Doc Partridge gave him were holding their own against the damned pain. Pausing in her knitting, Emily saw the direction of his gaze, fiercely glad she'd spent so much time and effort bringing Mary's garden back to life.

Soon shearing time was upon them, and even Charlie was busy mustering and yarding the sheep. The weather had improved, and so, one sunny morning Emily sat reading the newspapers to Hugh on the veranda. He usually enjoyed hearing all about Australia's latest successes in the Olympic Games down in Melbourne.

"Would have been fun for you to go, Em," he murmured drowsily. "I wonder if Vivienne Dalgleish appreciates her good fortune?"

Not likely, Emily thought, slightly ashamed of the spitefulness of her thoughts. *Vivienne takes such good fortune as her right.*

I tried to get one of those new-fangled television sets for you, Em," Hugh commented when Emily paused in her reading.

He still thought it a pity Geoff Johnson, of *Johnson's Emporium*, purveyors of anything and everything necessary to life on an outback station, had sold out. "Geoff said there'd been a run on them, what with everyone wanting to watch the Games," he added.

Which was the reason the residents of *Emu Downs* followed Australia's world-class team of Olympians via the radio and newspapers, while some of their neighbours watched the proceedings live on tiny screens in their living rooms.

When Hugh dozed off, Emily lay the paper aside. Lifting her face to the sun shining its benediction upon her, she soaked up the beauty of the place and the day, one hand resting lightly on her baby, now forming a rather large mound beneath her apron. It stirred, kicked vigorously, then rolled over and settled down again, bringing a radiant smile to Emily's face.

What with the warmth, the gentle drone of busy bees, and the perfume wafting up to her from the flowers, she dozed off herself, to be awakened by the cheerful carolling of magpies in the orchard beside the house. Stretching, she opened her eyes, gladdened when they fell on Ryan Farrelly riding by as he brought in another mob of sheep to be shorn, his dogs barking and snapping at the animals' heels to hurry them along.

Emily smiled with sheer joie de vivre, her heart singing.

Singing the song of a woman in love. A woman in love with the man she gazed upon.

Smile vanishing, Emily's hands closed on the arms of her chair, knuckles white from the desperate strength of her grip.

I can't be!

She couldn't be in love! Not with Ryan Farrelly who never gave her a second thought unless it was an uncomplimentary one. The scathing looks he sometimes cast her way told her he still considered her a callous gold-digger, despite his rather abrupt kindness to her.

Not to forget his preference for Vivienne Dalgleish.

Stop kidding yourself, Em, she thought. *Of course you are. You've been in love with the man for ages, only you've been too blind and too big a coward to admit it. All that big brother stuff was no more than a smokescreen to hide behind.*

"What's the matter, Em?"

Guilt struck Emily to the heart at Hugh's gentle question. She owed Hugh everything, especially her devotion and loyalty. That had been the essence of their bargain. For as long as he lived.

No! No! I can't be wishing Hugh's precious life away? What sort of horrible person am I?

At that moment the baby kicked again. Grateful for an unquestionable excuse, she lay her hand on her bulging belly. Her smile was a bit wobbly though, and she couldn't quite bring herself to meet Hugh's eyes.

"Nothing really. Baby was kicking a bit hard and caught me in a sensitive spot. I'm okay now."

This time when she smiled reassuringly at Hugh, she meant it. From the depths of her soul. Maybe she was in love with Ryan, but she also genuinely loved Hugh, with a daughter's love, and had pledged her loyalty to him.

Theirs was a contract she wouldn't be breaking. Ever. Not that she imagined she'd ever be offered the chance to. Even after Hugh was gone, she wouldn't stand a chance with Ryan.

Although he'd put a polite face on it for Hugh's sake, he'd made his disgust with her marriage, with her, all too plain. Also, in choosing to spend all his spare time with Vivienne, he'd made it abundantly clear his preference lay with the other woman.

No way would he be tempted to look *her* way.

As soon after Hugh's death as she could, she'd pack her bags and move out.

It was the only sensible thing to do. Until then, she'd keep her feelings to herself. It wouldn't be for much longer anyway. No amount of prayers could restore Hugh's health. Not when his heart had already gone ahead.

Tears were not far from the surface when she excused herself and went to her room for a few minutes until she was once more in control of her emotions.

EMILY'S BABY

9

Most evenings Ryan reported to Hugh, consulting on each day's schedule and on the coming week. Keeping the boss in the loop, even though he took progressively less interest in the daily workings of the property. Charlie, removed from the roster and replaced by another stockman, now worked close to the house every day; available if the women should need help attending to Hugh's personal needs. With Emily's advancing pregnancy, Hugh refused to let her do too much, and Joan was run off her feet with Hugh demanding so much of Emily's time.

Dr Partridge, taking it upon himself, arranged for Agnes Schaeffer, a private nurse, to move into the homestead, with a second nurse, Nina Santos, to relieve her on the night shifts. As spring progressed towards summer, and the days of Hugh's life drew to a close, an unconscious hush fell over the homestead. People spoke in softer voices. Joan was careful not to make a noisy clatter in the kitchen. The men changed into soft shoes inside the house. Even outside, the trill of birdsong sounded faintly muted.

The end came at the beginning of the first day of December.

Rising early, as had become her habit, to sit with her husband while Nina grabbed a cup of coffee, Emily quietly drew the curtains back, allowing Hugh to share the truly glorious sunrise heralding in the new day.

"Look Hugh," she smiled, drawing his attention to the celestial display. "It's going to be a beautiful day."

Obediently, Hugh turned his head on the pillow.

A beatific smile wreathed his sunken features. Without saying a word, he reached for Emily's hand.

As the colour faded from the sky, Emily felt his surprisingly firm grip slacken. His fingers fell open, releasing her from his hold. Looking down, she saw his eyes flutter closed. He emitted a single muffled sound, which in her heart she believed was the name of his beloved Mary, then he lay utterly still.

Nina arrived back to find Emily sitting by the bed, tears tracking silently down her cheeks.

"My dear," she whispered, taking in the scene with an expert eye. Hurrying forward, she lifted Hugh's unresponsive wrist, feeling for a pulse.

"He's gone, my dear." She gently lay his hand back at his side, turning her attention to the living. "Can I fetch anyone to you, or would you like a minute alone with him?"

Emily gave a little shiver, focusing on the motherly nurse at her side.

"I've already had my private moment, Nina. We watched the sunrise together." She reached into the pocket of her dressing gown for a handkerchief to wipe her eyes.

"Would you be a darling and phone Dr Partridge, then go and rouse the Duffys and Ryan? I'll sit here with him till they come."

Nina straightened the covers and lay Hugh's hands neatly upon his chest, then went to do Emily's bidding. Joan Duffy, already beginning the breakfast preparations, was there in a trice, but Ryan and Charlie had headed out to feed the animals as they did first thing every morning. Nina stepped outside to ring the bell on the veranda, summoning them back to the house.

Agnes, hearing the summoning bell and guessing its import, entered with her calm, stately tread, to join her colleague in Hugh's room.

Joan, who had been the household stalwart throughout the dark months, broke down, sobbing her heart out in her husband's arms. The men stood, stoically enduring pillars of support. None of the household seemed willing to be the first to introduce jarring practicality into these first minutes of grief. It was Agnes, feeling enough time had elapsed, who took charge of the situation.

"Why don't you go and get dressed, Emily?" she said, quietly taking the newly widowed young woman to one side. "You wouldn't want Dr Partridge to arrive and you still in your nightie, now, would you?"

"Perhaps you should ring Mr Blake's solicitor." Agnes next turned her attention to Ryan, the obvious man of the house now. "And Charlie, why don't you and Joan go and sit on the veranda for a few minutes? Nina will bring you a nice cup of tea."

She nodded the younger nurse towards the kitchen. "In fact, I think we can all do with a nice, strong cuppa."

In no time at all, she had the household organised. By the time Dr Partridge rattled over the cattle-grid, an air of spurious normalcy had settled upon the grieving household.

Packing quickly, the two nurses, not wishing to intrude, their time with this family having run its course, hitched a ride into town with the doctor. By lunch time only the Duffys, Ryan and Emily were left, sitting at the table toying with their food; even the undertaker having been and gone.

"I spoke with Harry Emden, Emily," Ryan reported. "He tells me Hugh organised all the details for the funeral several months ago. It's to be in two days' time, at ten in the morning. There's nothing for us to concern ourselves with except the reading of Hugh's will." His voice became gruffer as he continued. "There's to be a gathering at the pub, then the four of us are to attend Harry in his chambers."

"That's right, Ryan," Emily responded quietly. "Hugh didn't want us to be running around organising everything. He t ... told me ages ago that all we h ... had to do was phone Mr Emden." Emily took a few moments to pull herself together. "He'll even put the notices on the radio and in the newspapers. Hugh left me a list of people who merit a personal notification, though. I'll do that after lunch, if you can manage without me, Joan."

At Joan's assenting nod, Emily pushed her chair back, excusing herself from the table even though she'd barely touched her meal. She hurried down the hall to shut herself into the office, where she had a good cry before dialling the first number on Hugh's list.

The onerous task was almost completed when Joan sidled in with a cup of tea and an Anzac biscuit two hours later.

"Nearly finished, Em?" Emily smiled and stretched, glad of the interruption. Even gladder for the tea.

"Almost."

"Well, when you are," Joan continued, stern determination in every inch of her wiry figure, "you see that you take yourself off for a lie-down. Baby needs his Mum to take care of herself."

"I will, Joan." Reaching out for Joan's hand, she raised it to her cheek. "You're so good to me Joan. My mother couldn't have been nicer to me than you've been."

"Oh, go on with you, Emily." Joan's words might have brushed the compliment aside, but a rosy blush told another story.

I'm going to miss her so much when I leave. This time the tear Emily wiped from her eye was one of self-pity.

Instead of the lie-down Joan had ordered, Emily made a start on sorting what to keep. She planned to be gone before Christmas.

EMILY'S BABY

10

A bead of sweat trickled unpleasantly down the middle of Emily's back. Sitting front and centre at Hugh's graveside, the cynosure of all eyes, she couldn't even wriggle to ease her discomfort. Discomfort exacerbated by the churning and rolling motion of the baby.

Stoically, she held herself erect on the chair and tried to pay attention to Reverend Blaney as he droned his way through the burial service.

Just as she had sat stoically through the funeral service at All Saints Anglican Church a short time earlier.

A large number of Hugh's friends had spoken, all of them attesting to the man he had been. Wonderful though it was to hear their heart-warming anecdotes, to know how loved he'd been, each speaker had added to the length of the already long service.

Reverend Blayney didn't like to rush.

Ryan had spoken on behalf of the men employed on *Emu Downs*, and Joan Duffy had added a short testament of her own.

EMILY'S BABY

The heat in the tiny, tin-roofed church had risen alarmingly as the time approached midday, until Emily, feeling impatient for the service to be over, felt her hair becoming quite moist under her wide-brimmed black hat. Circles of perspiration, fortunately not immediately noticeable against the black linen suit she wore, had formed under her arms.

When her turn came to say a few words, she'd kept it short.

"Today marks the passing of a man who made friends wherever he went. A man who will be greatly missed by this community," she began. "Hugh told me once, that he considered himself blessed in his many friendships, and I know you will miss him dearly. As I will." She paused a moment to let her gaze roam around the packed church, including those who were forced by lack of space to stand at the back. "I loved him dearly. Hugh Blake was a kind, gentle man. A truly good man who invariably placed the needs of others ahead of his own. He will forever occupy a place of his own in my heart."

Baby gave a particularly hard kick. A wave of dizziness washed over her, and she sank gratefully back onto the front pew. Joan reached out to give her hand a sympathetic squeeze as Reverend Blayney brought the proceedings to a close and Ryan and the other five pallbearers carried the coffin down the aisle. Quite a few brows, and eyes, were moped as the congregation followed Emily and Joan in its wake, out to the blessed shade of a grove of peppercorn trees at the side of the church.

"Huh! Who does she think she's fooling with her pious pretence of being a grieving widow? Everyone knows she only married the old fool for his money."

Emily, caught up in the crowd of Hugh's friends paying their respects, reddened in anger, overhearing Irene Smythe's nasty comment to her long-suffering husband. About to turn and retaliate, she felt her arm gripped tightly, and glared at her friend, Susan Brandon who held her back. Her honour didn't go unavenged, however.

"And what would you know, Irene Smythe?" Joan Duffy responded hotly. "I've lived in the same house for months, and nobody could have been more loving and caring than our Emily."

"Come on." Ryan was suddenly at Emily's side, steering her towards where the car was drawn up close to the lychgate. "Charlie," he uttered quietly above her head, "fetch Joan out of there before we've got a cat-fight on our hands."

Almost over.

Plucking her damp skirt away from her legs, Emily stood for the last hymn. Leading the procession past the open grave a few minutes later, she kept on walking after tossing her handful of dirt onto the coffin.

"Please. Can we just go straight to the *Southern Cross*?" she pleaded. The weight of the baby pressing down on her bladder was unbearable; added to which, she felt nauseous from the heat. "I need some time to myself."

Just one more thing, then we can go home.

The refreshments and talk at the hotel were taking forever, and there was still the will to be read.

All Emily wanted was to lie down in her own cool bedroom, with the blinds drawn, back on *Emu Downs*. For this interminable day to be over. Her back ached something awful. Her head ached; and her bladder was making itself felt yet again. Almost out the door she was stopped once more.

"My sincerest sympathy, Mrs Blake," Brad Dalgleish said, taking her hand in his as he spoke. "Anything we can do, all you need to do is ask. I know my wife would second me if she were here. Such a pity she is away and not able to offer her support."

"Thank you, Mr Dalgleish," Emily responded, noting he hadn't mentioned his daughter.

Perhaps that would be stretching the truth too far.

With other things occupying her mind lately, she hadn't been paying attention to the gossip, but now she recalled an overheard conversation between Joan and Barbara Elliot.

It seemed the Dalgleish ladies had joined some friends in a hastily organised trip to England. Rumour had it Vivienne had attracted the attention of a titled visitor to the Games in Melbourne, and was following him home. "Striking while the iron's hot," Joan had summed it up. Emily hoped Vivienne's quest proved successful. She hoped the dratted woman was out of their hair for good. *Out of Ryan's hair,* she thought. *He deserves better.*

She shook Brad Dalgleish 's hand, then continued on her way without further interruptions.

"Time to go, Em." Charlie and Joan were waiting for her outside the restroom when she emerged. "Ryan's bringing the car round."

"Thank God." Emily stretched her back, then hauled the hat off her head and ran her fingers through her damp hair.

Ten minutes later Harry Emden was ushering her into an armchair across from his desk. Ryan and the Duffys, the only others invited to the reading of the will, settled on either side of her.

Since Hugh had made her fully aware of who was to receive what, she would willingly have skipped this formality, but the others deserved to hear how much Hugh had valued them, so she prepared herself for another period of discomfort in Harry Emden's stuffy office.

Why, she had wondered silently, *do lawyers have to have their offices on the second storey?* Hauling her bulk up the stairs, had almost been too much for her.

"I can see you're feeling the heat, Mrs Blake," Harry said, "so I'll make this as quick as I can."

He donned his reading glasses, cleared his throat, and tapped the manila folder on his desk.

"Right, people. Let's get started." He opened the folder.

"First up, Hugh was of sound mind when he made this will. Dr Partridge has signed a note to say so. Not that I imagine anyone present is likely to try and contest it. Waste of time if you did. It's sown up watertight."

His audience had nothing to say, so he cleared his throat again and began reading. After the preliminaries came a long list of charitable donations.

"Hugh told me he discussed these with you, Mrs Blake."

"Yes, Mr Emden. He did."

"Right. Now we come to the serious stuff. Mr and Mrs Duffy."

Harry looked at them over the top of his glasses.

"You've both been employed at *Emu Downs* for many years. Hugh considered you his friends. Thinking you might like to remain in the district after you retire, he's left you ten thousand pounds and the house at ..." He rattled off the address on the best street in St Denis.

"Oh!" Joan gasped, clapping her hands over her mouth. "Oh, but I never expected anything like that!"

"Mighty generous," Charlie muttered, fishing for his handkerchief to dab at his eyes.

"Mrs Blake. You're next. Hugh said to explain that he's not mentioned the baby specifically, since he trusts you implicitly to take care of its interests."

"Yes, Mr Emden. He explained that to me."

"He wasn't sure if you'd want to stay in the outback or not, so he's left you the six holiday houses at Bateman's Bay, which bring in a very tidy sum each year."

Emily nodded to indicate she knew this too.

"As well, you're to get half of his investment portfolio and any monies remaining after the disbursement of funds following probate. I expect there'll be a tidy sum involved."

This time it was Emily who gasped and covered her mouth. That was a lot more than Hugh had led her to believe he was giving her.

"There's more, but we'll leave that for a bit. Mr Farrelly. Hugh told me you were like a second son to him, and that he'd made you a verbal promise to leave *Emu Downs* to you. He's done just that, along with the other half of the investment portfolio as a cushion against a bad season while you're getting yourself established."

Ryan lifted his head abruptly, then reddened. After all the hard things he'd thought, Hugh hadn't forgotten his promise.

"He did say something of the kind, but that was before his marriage. I never dared think he'd remember it."

"It was one of the first things Hugh mentioned when he explained his will to me," Emily said, smiling at Ryan. She liked that he hadn't taken Hugh's favour for granted.

"Right," Harry said once again.

"Almost there now. One last thing, and it concerns all of you."

He allowed himself a prim little smile when all four people seated in front of him frowned, looking bewildered. He reckoned this item was the bombshell in an otherwise straightforward will.

"Hugh didn't want you disappearing into the sunset as soon as he was under the ground, Emily. Not with a new baby, and I can see you've not much longer to wait. He wanted you to stay on *Emu Downs* where you're comfortable, for one year after his death. At least one year. Therefore, the homestead, and the gardens inside the paling fence, are yours for as long as you want them." He looked up, smiling in appreciation at the stunned expressions on everyone's faces.

"If you decide to leave, the house will revert to being included once again with the rest of the property, thereby becoming Mr Farrelly's. The entire contents of the house, however, will remain your property, Mrs Blake, to be taken with you should you choose to keep them if you leave. So there's no unseemly gossip, Mrs Blake," Harry frowned severely over the top of his glasses,

"Hugh asks Mr and Mrs Duffy, as a favour to him, to stay on with Mrs Blake for this period of one year, instead of immediately taking your retirement, which you are, however, fully entitled to do."

"And a good thing too," Joan declared. "Of course we'll be staying. As long as you need us, Emily. This is an excellent idea of Hugh's. The last thing you want to be doing, Emily, is moving house with a new baby. Much better to leave it a while." *Better still,* she thought to herself, *is not to leave at all.* She could see a perfectly simple solution to Emily's future, if only the young people could be persuaded to act on it.

Harry Emden adjusted his glasses and cleared his throat.

"Last item on the agenda. Hugh left letters for all of you, to be read when you're on your own." He handed out four letters in sealed envelopes. "Does anyone have any questions?"

No questions occurred to anyone, so Harry wound up the proceedings smartly enough to satisfy even Emily, who was more uncomfortable than ever. The baby felt as if it was trying to kick its way out of her. Tucking her letter safely into her handbag, she slipped into the restroom at the head of the stairs outside Harry's office.

Her muffled scream turned all heads towards the door.

Emily, ashen-faced, staggered out of the restroom a moment later.

"Mr Emden, I'm so sorry. I've made an awful mess in here. I think my waters broke." A stricken look on her face, she stared at her friends.

"I think the baby's coming."

EMILY'S BABY

11

Without warning, Emily fell back against the wall, clutching her mountainous baby bulge. An agonised shriek startled everyone, as she sobbed, unable to control the wave of pain tearing her apart. If this was the labour pain she'd heard so much about, she didn't think she could bear it. She wanted it to stop.

Pandemonium reigned.

Surprisingly, it was Charlie Duffy who restored a modicum of calm.

He took Emily in his arms, patting her comfortingly on the back.

"I'm the eldest of nine kids," he told her. "I had to step up a time or two and help my Mum when the little ones arrived. Oh, not the actual delivery!" He sounded just as shocked at the very thought as the other two men looked. "The midwife always arrived in time, but I remember this bit really well."

He turned his attention back to where it was needed. In keeping Emily calm.

"You'll be fine, Girl. Just a bit of a shock, starting like that when you weren't expecting it."

"But it's too early," Joan protested. "It's not due till next month. There must be something wrong."

"Now, now, Joanie. Don't go alarming the lass. Babies come to their own timetable, not ours, and it's been an upsetting few days, besides."

About to correct Joan, Emily remembered Hugh's little subterfuge about the due date, and closed her mouth. If it hadn't been for the funeral, she might not have been taken by surprise.

This baby was right on time.

Ryan stood there, watching helplessly. As useless as Joan and Harry. Give him a horse or sheep and he'd be right at home, but a human baby ... Emily's baby ... He thanked God for Charlie. At least Emily had *someone* she could rely on.

"Let's get going before the next contraction hits," Charlie said, his arm still around Emily's shoulders.

"Harry, you get on the phone and let the hospital know we're on our way. They'll call Doc Partridge. Joan, run down to the car and fetch that old towel from the boot. Fold it up and put it on the front seat for Em to sit on. She won't want to muck up the leather, will you girl?" He smiled down at Emily, receiving a wobbly smile in return.

"Ryan, give me a hand here, Mate. Let's give Em a lift down the stairs."

At last. Something he could do.

Ryan stepped forward with alacrity to join Charlie. The men made a chair with their arms and carried Emily down the steep, narrow flight of stairs, arriving at the bottom just as the next contraction hit. Better prepared this time, Emily managed to contain her instinctive scream, muting it to a gasping moan.

"Breathe, Emily!" Charlie commanded. "Breathe your way through it. Ride the pain. Come on, Girl. You can do it."

She found she could. This was what Agnes had said, too, when Emily had appealed to the nurse for advice.

The next contraction, lasting longer than the previous two, struck as they pulled into the hospital carpark.

"Inside, Joanie, and fetch help," Charlie ordered, flinging open the front door to hold Emily and coach her through it again. Two nurses and an orderly pushing a gurney, rushed up to them. Elbowing Charlie out of their way, they immediately took charge, carefully lifting Emily onto the gurney and covering her with a sheet.

"The little one's in a bit of a hurry, seems like, Sister. Five minutes apart and lasting a bit longer each time," Charlie reported. The sister nodded her appreciation, and hurried her party through the emergency entrance, taking Emily's pulse as she strode along at her side.

Charlie pushed back his hat to wipe his brow, then reached for his tobacco and began skilfully rolling a cigarette.

"Thank God you were there, Charlie," Ryan muttered, still looking rather dazed. "None of the rest of us had a bloody clue." He watched Charlie rolling his smoke.

"Don't suppose you've got another of those, have you Mate? Need something to steady my nerves."

He held out hands which had a slight tremor. Charlie chuckled and held out the finished cigarette, rolling a second one for himself. Joan arrived to see the men; heads close together as Charlie shared a match with Ryan.

"Can't you find anything better to do than stand around smoking?" she berated them. "Emily might be needing us. What'll she think if we're not there?"

"Calm down, Old Girl." Her husband wrapped his arm around her in a comforting hug.

"Even babies in a hurry take a while. We'll just finish our smokes, then I reckon we oughta find ourselves a cup of tea." A few minutes later, both cigarettes were being thoroughly stubbed out underfoot. The men straightened, turning towards the entrance with Joan chivvying them along.

"Hang on a mo."

Charlie about turned, ignoring Joan's impatient, "Come on."

"Just remembered something. Didn't Em have a suitcase packed ready. I seem to recall seeing it taking up space in the boot. Better get it. She'll be wanting it before the day's out."

"Oh my God, yes." Joan clapped both hands over her mouth. "That Agnes Schaeffer helped her get her stuff together. She told her to keep it in the boot, since we'd be bringing her in by car when the time came."

"Well, the time's come, hasn't it?" Ryan muttered. He strode past them to retrieve the case. Slamming the boot shut, he led the way inside, suitcase in hand.

After that came the waiting.

Ryan paced.

Joan fretted.

Charlie sneaked outside for another smoke, arriving back with fresh cups of tea all round.

And they waited.

Finally, seven and a half hours after Emily's waters broke in Harry Emden's office, Dr Partridge stepped into the waiting room, becoming the immediate focus of their attention.

"We have a little girl," he announced, "and mother and baby are both well. Very well," he emphasised. "The nurses are tidying Mrs Blake up, then, when she's back in her room, you can have five minutes before you go home." He smiled benignly at them, then wandered off down the corridor.

*****

"Oh, Em. She's a real little darling," Joan gushed. "Sister gave us a peek through the nursery window." She threw her arms around her young friend, giving her a smacking kiss on the cheek.

Charlie, right behind her, was a little more restrained with his fatherly buss on her other cheek.

"You've done well, Emmy-lass," he told her, a grin splitting his face from ear to ear. He stepped back to allow Ryan a turn to offer his own congratulations.

If it's good enough for Joan and Charlie ... Ryan seized his opportunity to steal a hug and a kiss on Emily's cheek.

"You have a beautiful baby, Emily. Hugh would have been very proud of you both."

His comment brought a tear to Emily's eye, but, wiping it away with a corner of the sheet, she refused to let sorrow dim her joy. There'd be plenty of time to grieve; tonight, she'd rejoice. She smiled mistily at her friends.

"Whatcha gonna call her?" Charlie wanted to know. "Picked out a name, have you?"

Emily nodded.

"I have. She's going to be Andrea-Maree after Hugh's Mary and Andrew. And Charlie, I think I'll add Charlotte for you. You were such a comfort this afternoon."

Charlie was still puffed up with pride when Sister came to send them on their way.

"Baby's being named after me, Sister. Andrea-Maree Charlotte Blake. Whadda you think of that!"

*****

Two days later, Susan Brandon was admitted to the second bed in Emily's bed, proud mother of another little girl.

"I reckon our girls will grow up best friends, Em. I was thinking of Andrea myself, since my husband's an Andrew, only you got in first," she laughed.

"Sorry," Emily smiled. She felt a little guilty for letting Sue assume she'd be staying on *Emu Downs* forever. Not that she didn't want to. She loved the farm, but it wasn't hers. Even the house was only hers for the next year. She turned away, a shadow crossing her face at the thought of the future.

Not wanting to dampen Susan's happiness, she fixed a determined smile on her face and demanded to be told the new baby's name.

"So, what name have you decided on?"

"Oh, Andy and I settled for Simone for his father, and Barbara for Mum."

EMILY'S BABY

12

Without Susan, the time spent in the hospital would have been lonely for Emily. The strictly supervised visiting hours each afternoon and evening passed far too quickly for all the questions she wanted to ask, and all she had saved up to share. Joan, her most frequent visitor, was too busy to make the long drive in from the farm twice daily, and although Charlie and Ryan took turns coming in the evenings, it still left a great many hours when Emily's mind filled with memories of Hugh. Hours when she was in danger of lapsing into melancholy.

He would have so loved to see little Andrea-Maree.

Didi, Emily amended, *Andrea-Maree is too much of a mouthful for every-day.* Her heart overflowed with love for the baby suckling at her breast, one tiny fist clenched firmly around her mother's finger. *If only …*

Naming her baby Andrea Maree was a tribute to Hugh, without whose generosity she would most likely have been forced to give the precious mite up for adoption. She owed him everything, but still, she would use the diminutive, Didi.

I'm sure Hugh would have been the first to agree, she told herself.

Looking across to the second bed in the private ward where Sue Brandon was similarly occupied with her Simone, Emily called out softly.

"Sue." When her friend glanced up, a dreamy new-mother smile softening her features, Emily continued. "I've decided to shorten Andrea to Didi. What do you think?" She held her breath, waiting anxiously for Sue's reaction.

"Didi? Didi Blake. I like it, Em. It has a distinctive ring to it."

Emily let go of her pent-up breath, smiling in relief.

"You don't think anyone will be offended, do you?"

"Whatever for? Most babies named after someone get their name shortened to save confusion, if for no other reason."

If her arms weren't already full, Emily would have rushed over and hugged her friend for her forthright common sense. It was a pity she'd be leaving soon. She'd never felt so in tune with a girlfriend of her own age, and really would have liked to have Sue for a close, life-long friend.

But I don't have to leave. Not unless I really want to.

Suddenly a whole new vista opened up before her. *With the money Hugh left me, I can live wherever I choose. It doesn't have to be a choice between Emu Downs or Sydney.*

She turned her attention back to Didi, but the idea returned to the forefront of her mind once the babies had been returned to the nursery and Sue had padded off to the bathroom for a refreshing shower.

She fished Hugh's farewell letter out of her handbag where it had languished unread, ever since she'd stuffed it there when Harry Emden handed it to her. Overtaken by events, she'd almost forgotten it. Opening it carefully, she extracted several sheets covered with Hugh's distinctive handwriting and smoothed them out. She skimmed through it quickly, gasping in some places, and chuckling to herself in others; then she read it again. Slowly, this time; taking in every word he'd written to her.

The changes to his will, which had taken her by surprise, were explained more fully, and he reiterated the reasons he felt she shouldn't be in too big a hurry to leave *Emu Downs*. With one notable addition he hadn't confided in Harry Emden to be passed on. Emily thought it over for a minute or two, her heart pounding in her breast, then she returned to that particular passage and read it again.

'... and I have one more reason I'd like you to spend a few more months here, Emily, my dear. You're a young woman with your whole life ahead of you. I'm sure you'll fall in love and marry again – a good man who'll love you in return. You've gained in maturity quite a bit this year, and I'm sure you'll choose wisely; which will make me very happy for you.

Right now, you're probably not thinking that far ahead, but you need a decent man by your side, and Baby will need a good father. I might even be able to steer you towards that good, decent man.

I've noticed the way Ryan Farrelly watches you when he thinks no-one is looking. He gives every appearance of being very strongly attracted. To you, Emily; and you're free now to reciprocate if you've a mind to. Please stay long enough for his feelings to deepen, now he's not restrained by my presence.'

Was Hugh right? She'd always thought Ryan merely tolerated her for Hugh's sake. That was certainly the case when she first arrived, and he'd never given her cause to believe his feelings towards her had warmed. As Hugh obviously believed they had.

Did she want Hugh to be right?

She put her hand over her heart, noting it was beating much faster than normal. A blush warmed her cheeks.

Oh, yes I do! she answered herself. It had been a long while since she realised just how much she was attracted to Ryan. Hiding her feelings had taken a considerable effort. *And I'll continue to hide them, too. Until I know for sure what his are. Then I'll know whether to pack up and leave Emu Downs or not.*

Her mind calm now she'd reached a decision, she folded her letter carefully and returned it to the security of her handbag.

Fancy Hugh matchmaking for me from his grave, she giggled, scooping up her toiletries and towel for her turn under the shower.

She couldn't help wondering if Hugh had given Ryan a similar prompt in the letter he'd left for him.

*****

Both Emily and Susan were allowed to take their babies home in plenty of time to help their households prepare for Christmas. A wholly joyous occasion for Susan. One tinged with sadness for her friend. On the morning of their last day together in the private maternity ward, they exchanged the small gifts they had for each other and their babies. Gifts left wrapped and labelled at home and smuggled in by their visitors.

Joan had collected Emily and Didi after Dr Partridge made his rounds, giving them a clean bill of health and discharging them.

"Oh, Joan, you can't imagine how good it feels to be going home at last. We've got so much to do before Christmas."

"I didn't think you'd want to be fussing with a big celebration so soon after Hugh's death." Joan pursed her lips disapprovingly, her tone definitely acidic. "The dear man's still warm in his grave."

"I didn't mean celebrating Christmas as in partying, Joan. Surely you didn't think that." Emily wasn't going to be cowed into an exaggerated show of grief just to satisfy the older woman's idea of correct behaviour.

"There'll be no parties, of course, but it *is* Christmas. Didi's first Christmas. I think we should put up a tree and some decorations. She won't remember, but if we take photos, she can look at them when she's older. We can still have presents and Christmas dinner without being disrespectful to Hugh. You know he'd want us to carry on as normally as possible."

Joan nodded slowly, so, as a clincher, Emily added,

"He told me so in the letter he left for me."

"In mine too," Joan grudgingly conceded.

"I'll be going to the early morning church service, if you'd like to join me." Emily had already planned to make this trip early on Christmas morning, but mentioned it now, hoping to mollify Joan, who nodded again, her expression lighter now she realised she'd misjudged Emily.

"There ought to be enough flowers in the garden to take a bunch for Hugh. Matron let me walk down to the cemetery yesterday, you know, and I took him all the flowers people had brought me. There were others already there as well. They looked to be from our garden. Thank you for that, Joan." Emily reached over and patted Joan on the shoulder.

"I really miss him," Joan wailed, sniffing back a sob. "Now see what you've gone and done," she accused, "I can't be carrying on like this while I'm driving." Slowing down to a crawl on the deserted road, she fumbled a handkerchief from her pocket and blew her nose. Restored to normal, she pressed down on the accelerator again. It seemed no time at all before they rattled over the cattle-grid in front of the homestead.

Ryan and Charlie leaned on the veranda rail, waiting for them. As soon as the car pulled up at the foot of the steps, they came down. While Charlie went to the boot to unload Emily's bags, Ryan opened the passenger door of the car, reaching in to take Didi from her mother.

"Welcome home, Emily. Let me take this young lady so you can get out."

"Trust you to get in first for a cuddle," Charlie complained. "That starchy sister wouldn't let us any closer than the viewing window in the nursery. 'Hospital policy', she said. Bloody stupid policy if you ask me. Babies can't ever get too many cuddles. Especially fatherless ones like our babe."

"You'll both get plenty of chances for cuddles," Joan brought her husband's grumbles to a halt. "Get those bags inside, why don't you, Charlie Duffy."

Her sharper than usual tone to the husband she adored made Emily stare at her, a tiny frown creasing her brow. Something was up with Joan, only she couldn't imagine what. She'd put her snippiness in the car down to the grief she undoubtedly felt, but now she began thinking there might be more to it.

"If you give Didi back to me, Ryan, I'll go along with Charlie. Madame needs a change and a feed."

Right on cue, the baby began fussing. Ryan, suddenly detecting a strong odour coming from his cuddly armful, gingerly handed her back.

"Well, as to that, ..." Charlie began, more diffidently than his usual forthright utterances. He trailed off, leaving Emily staring at him now as he shuffled his feet, eyes on the ground. She looked at Ryan, who also looked ill-at-ease. Finally, she turned to Joan. What was wrong with everybody today? She'd expected a warm, happy homecoming with baby Didi. Instead she felt almost as if they didn't want her there.

The men both looked to Joan. Casting them both a scathing glance, she lifted her head in what Emily could have sworn was a defiant gesture and accepted the challenge.

"The thing is, Emily," Joan began, drawing the girl's attention to herself, "we ... I decided to make a few changes. Hugh said to, in his letter to me," she elucidated, "so I cleared out his room and moved your things into it. The room you used to have is back to being a nursery. What it was originally meant to be." She finished with a rush, chin raised, staring Emily in the eye.

Emily stiffened. Angry colour flooded her face. She was on the point of giving Joan a serve about minding her own business, when Charlie jumped in to deflect her annoyance from his wife.

"Hugh didn't want you to have to bother yourself with a whole lot of extra stuff on your own. He asked Joanie to help."

"We all helped." Ryan, arms folded across his chest, aligned himself with the other two.

"I reckon we made a good job of it, Emily. We stripped off all that old-fashioned dark wallpaper and painted your room in nice light colours. Joan swapped out the curtains and bedding for some from the spare room across the hall. The mattress too. It looks completely different now. You've got more space than being crammed into the small room with Didi. If you don't like it, you can get it redone."

His explanation had given Emily time to get her temper under control. She really, really didn't want to get into a row with any of them. Slowly, she gazed from one tense face to the other. They didn't either, she realised. This was what had been worrying Joan all the way home from town. She took a deep breath and forced herself to smile. It wasn't her best smile, but a smile nonetheless.

"Thank you. All of you." They relaxed, and Emily's smile grew warmer as the danger faded.

"Hugh said something of the same to me, too. I should have talked to you about my plans, Joan, but it sounds as if you've saved me a whole load of work. What did you do with Hugh's things?"

"They're all boxed up in the spare room," Joan said. "I would never take the liberty of disposing of so much as a handkerchief without consulting you first, Emily. We just wanted to do something special to help you. I'm sorry if I overstepped."

Not so much as a handkerchief, but it was alright to turn my rooms upside down and inside out.

Realising she'd be foolish to make any more of it, Emily shrugged lightly.

"It's okay, Joan. Now, if there are no more surprises, I really have to attend to Didi." During the last few minutes, the baby had gone from fussing to a lusty, demanding howl.

"I'll bring you a nice cup of tea."

"That would be super, Joan. I'm dying for a cup."

Alone in the room which had once been Hugh's and was now hers, Emily gazed about her in wonderment. Not only had the colour-scheme and bedding been changed; the furniture had been rearranged as well. Comparing before and after, it was hard to believe this was the same room. The only unchanged feature was the view through the window. Across the garden and the dam, over the paddocks to the woodland on the crest of the rise, it was the same view as she'd had from the adjoining room. A view she'd grown to love.

EMILY'S BABY

13

"We need to talk, Emily."

Ryan leaned forward to speak softly over Emily's shoulder when he eased her chair back as she rose from the table after dinner. Emily wanted to discuss several matters with him, too, only he had disappeared back outside by the time she'd settled Didi and gone to find her own belated lunch. She wouldn't feel entirely comfortable until they'd discussed the changes instigated by Hugh's death and his surprising will.

"We do," she agreed. "Do you mind if we sit on the front veranda, Ryan? I can hear Didi from there if she wakes up early."

"I'll bring coffee out," Joan offered, correctly assuming Ryan would have no objection. "Then, I think Charlie and I will have an early night, as soon as I've washed the dishes."

"Oh, Joan, what am I thinking, leaving you with all the cleaning up!"

"As if I can't handle a few dishes," Joan scoffed. "I know Ryan wants to sort out a few important issues before our little girl demands her Mama again. Shoo!"

Laughing, Emily followed Ryan to the chairs on the front veranda, where Joan brought them the coffee tray almost before they were settled.

Ryan had asked for the meeting, so Emily waited expectantly after pouring the coffee.

"Emily," he began, tentatively choosing his words. "You must be disappointed with Hugh giving *Emu Downs* to me …"

"Not at all!" Emily broke in, quick to reassure him.

"I've told you before, Ryan. Hugh and I discussed all of that months ago. We both agreed it would be best for *Emu Downs* if you were left in charge. I'd be in a right pickle if running this place was up to me."

"That's all very well, but you're his wife. You and Didi should have been left everything. If you want to contest the will, I won't stand in your way."

Even though it would break his heart to say goodbye to his dreams.

"I won't be doing anything of the sort! Didi and I have all we need. More than I expected, really."

Emily debated with herself whether or not to tell Ryan the truth about her marriage, but if she decided to stay in the area as she was considering, she didn't want any stray words leaking out to sully her daughter's standing. Or discredit herself, after Hugh's careful manipulation of the facts.

No, she decided. *Unless the future Hugh had hinted at eventuates, I'll tell no-one. Not even a man as honourable as Ryan Farrelly.*

"If you're sure, then." His sigh of relief didn't go unmissed by his companion. "I'll get my gear together tomorrow and move down to the men's quarters."

"Whatever for?" This time he really had taken her by surprise.

"The house is yours, Emily. There'll be talk if I don't get out of your way."

"Oh, rubbish! Why do you think Hugh asked the Duffys to stay on? Your room isn't even in the main house. It's in the new wing built for housing the jackaroos, only we don't have any. I'd like to see anybody accuse Joan Duffy of turning a blind eye to 'goings on' as she put it."

"But ..."

"Don't be silly Ryan. This is your home; just as it always has been, and will be after I leave." Emily didn't miss the surprise which flashed over his face when she said that. Or the tightening of his mouth which followed. Though whether that signified good for her, or otherwise, she couldn't tell. He was hard to read when his face assumed its stoic look, shutting in his emotions.

"You're staying; and that's that!" she declared.

Once again Ryan allowed himself to be persuaded to do what he really wanted to do.

"Do you have any more silly notions, Ryan?" He mutely shook his head.

This new, assertive Emily came as a surprise to him. On top of Hugh's letter, refuting all allegations of her being any kind of scheming gold-digger, he was beginning to revise the initial view of her which he'd clung to in self-defence for so long.

He recalled Hugh's subtle hint at an eminently satisfactory method of resolving any guilt feelings he might have at depriving Emily of her full right of inheritance, and sat a little straighter. Hugh had given him a green light to follow through on his attraction to the girl. And he was half-inclined to admit the idea had its appeal. He turned in his chair to face her, opening his mouth to say … What?

His mouth dried. What if the attraction was one-sided? He'd better not stick his neck out till he could be a little more certain of his reception.

Emily, who'd been gazing out across the dam, suddenly swung to face him.

"While we're talking, Ryan, there's a couple of items I need to clarify. Charlie Duffy told me he's retiring from station work. He's just going to help around the gardens and with the household animals, although, he said if you need an extra pair of hands you can always call on him. So you can take both Duffys off the station payroll. I'll pay their wages from now on."

This time it was Ryan who broke in before Emily finished.

"There's no need for that. If I'm to stay here, Joan will be cooking and cleaning for me, so I ought to be the one paying her."

"I checked with Mr Emden," Emily huffed.

"He agreed with me. Come to a private arrangement with Joan if you like, but she works in the house, which is my responsibility for as long as I'm here."

Ryan grunted a grudging assent, causing Emily to narrow her eyes at him.

"And that's another thing. I'm really glad I don't have to move out immediately, but if you want me to go earlier than the year Hugh suggested, please tell me, Ryan. I don't want to make life difficult for you."

"Can't see any reason I'd want you to. I've got used to having you around, and I can't see young Didi being a problem."

"Okay then. Last item on my list. Mr Emden says the Holden belongs to the property. I'll order a new one for Joan and myself to use, but in the meantime, can we borrow it when we need to go out?"

"Of course you can. No need to buy anything new, either. I can use the ute if you women want the Holden. Consider it payment in kind for my continued residency."

Although half inclined to argue the point, Emily decided to let Ryan have the last word. She poured herself a second cup and topped his off as well. Leaning back, she watched a near-full moon rising over the ridge, it's light almost obliterating the stars which were beginning to appear. She gave a heartfelt sigh.

"Thanks for making it easy, Ryan. I really do love living here. I know there's no way I can stay forever, but when I do leave, I doubt I'll go far."

Well, that was one of his questions answered. Tempted to hint at his growing feelings for her, Ryan held back.

The girl had buried her husband only days ago. He might not understand much about her marriage, but every day since she'd arrived on Hugh's arm, she'd clearly demonstrated a genuine love for him. It would be altogether too crass of him to make a move on her until a bit more water flowed under the bridge.

Neither felt the need to say more, however there was nothing awkward about the silence between them. In fact, Emily felt a companionable warmth, drinking coffee and watching the moonrise together. A regretful sigh issued from her lips when she heard her baby stirring.

14

Where once the Duffys, habitually retiring to their own rooms after dinner to read or listen to the radio, had left Emily to keep Hugh company, now it was Ryan in whose company they left her for an hour or two each evening.

A cosy domesticity developed between Ryan and herself. Some nights they discussed farm issues and local news items over their after-dinner coffee. At other times Ryan would bring out the cards or the chessboard and, with a great deal of laughter distracting them from their game, they'd battle to the death with the radio playing quietly in the background.

Entertaining themselves never seemed a problem, and Emily found herself looking forward to these shared hours more and more. Knowing there was no longer any reason to suppress her liking, more than liking even, for the attractive young farmer, she relaxed in his company as she never had before. Although neither she nor Ryan ever crossed the invisible line separating Hugh's widow and his best friend, with increasing frequency there were times when a certain awareness in Ryan's eyes raised a blush in Emily's cheeks.

Or when an accidental brushing of hands would make her pulse accelerate and an exciting warmth invade the mysterious lower regions of her body.

Times when Ryan's self-imposed role of caring older brother would lapse, leaving Emily in no doubt he saw her as a desirable woman. Only she was too inexperienced, and too fearful of being seen to dishonour Hugh's memory so soon after his death, to know how to take advantage of those lapses.

It was really difficult being a supposedly experienced woman, married, widowed and now a mother, whose sole experience of sex had been one shameful, furtive episode she'd prefer to forget.

Why, I'm almost a virgin, she thought. *It would be so much easier if I was. Then I could simply be myself. But if I were, I wouldn't even be here with Ryan.*

The role imposed upon her by her marriage to Hugh sometimes weighed very heavily indeed. How she wished her mother was still alive to go to for advice. These were issues she'd be too ashamed to discuss with any of the new friends she'd made; even Susan Brandon whom she felt she could trust with most confidences.

*****

It was near the end of January when Joan brought the newspaper to the table one evening, slipping it beneath her chair with a defiant challenge in the tilt of her chin. She waited till the last spoonful of peach Melba had been swallowed before she brought it out, already turned back at the entertainment page.

"It says here that musical film, *Carousal*, is coming to St Denis this weekend. You know, I do love a good musical, Charlie. Do you think it's too soon to go to something like this?" She gazed commandingly round the table. "Only, if we miss out now, who knows if we'll ever get another chance to see it?"

A sparkle lit up Emily's eyes. Twisting her hands together out of sight in her lap, she allowed herself to hope. They had been in the habit of attending the local cinema quite regularly, but she hadn't had a night out in months. Not since Hugh entered the final stages of his illness, and oh, how she'd appreciate an excuse to dress up and break out of the rut, comfortable though it was, she'd settled into.

Dancing was out of the question, but the movies …

If the Duffys go, maybe … She listened with bated breath.

"I reckon something like that ought to be okay." It was Charlie who spoke up, all eyes turning to him as he delivered his considered opinion.

"Tell you what, Joanie old girl, let's have dinner at *The Southern Cross*, then take in the movies. You haven't had a night off in ages."

"Good idea, Charlie," Ryan briskly seconded. "We'll all go. You and I as well, Emily. You've earned a treat, too, and I can't see how anyone could possibly have the slightest objection."

"Ryan's right, Emily," Joan agreed. "You do deserve a treat."

"Didi?"

"She's a good little thing. If you sit beside the aisle near the back you can step out with her if she fusses. I've seen other women do that."

"So have I, Joan. I'll do it." Emily clasped her hands in front of her with a breathless little laugh, reminding the other three just how very young she actually was, despite being both a widow and a mother. A reminder which sat heavily upon Ryan's conscience.

That evening when Emily brought their coffee through after helping Joan clear away, she found Ryan in the farm office, open ledgers strewn across the desk.

"Oh. Thanks, Emily. Just leave mine here, would you?" Without looking at her, he cleared a spot on the desk. "I've got some paperwork to catch up on."

Looking forward to discussing the upcoming trip to the movies with him, Emily was somewhat taken aback by his aloof, slightly distant manner. It had been her impression he enjoyed their evenings together as much as she did, but he was sending out unmistakeable signals that her presence was not required. Disconsolately, she put his cup down in the space he'd cleared, then silently retreated to the veranda. Alone.

Oh well, she shrugged, picking up her cup to take a sip, *maybe he really is busy, and that's all it is.*

Enjoying the refreshing coolness of evening after yet another sweltering day, she let her mind drift along more pleasurable lines. Her old, pre-baby clothes didn't fit very well any more, but there was a new outfit, just the thing for Saturday night, hanging in her wardrobe.

In crease-resistant navy-blue, the sombre colour, along with black gloves, a concession to her bereaved state, it had a swing skirt which showed her legs to advantage, and a front-buttoning peplum blouse in the same fabric.

It was loose enough to modestly accommodate breasts fuller than previously, courtesy of Didi.

Joan had been very complimentary when she'd modelled it for her. Continuing her mental fashion parade, Emily added her pearl brooch and matching pearl earrings. They would set the outfit off to perfection.

In spite of being abandoned to her own devices, there was a cheerful smile on her face when she answered Didi's cry for attention.

When, the following evening, Ryan was once again his usual self, trouncing her at poker which he'd been teaching her to play, she let go of the niggling question which had disturbed her peace off and on during the day. A disproportionate relief flooded her being at realising nothing was wrong between them after all. Ryan had been distant with her because he was busy, and for no other reason.

The movies excursion was a resounding success. When the *Emu Downs* party trooped into *The Southern Cross* dining room, Barbara Elliot, seated at a neighbouring table with several friends, settled her smiling gaze on Emily, carefully assessing her dress and demeanour. Returning the younger woman's greeting with a discreet nod of approval, she returned her attention to her own meal, and Emily relaxed.

Didi, good baby that she was, dozed off in her mother's arms during the newsreels and cartoons which had been followed by a rip-roaring western, full of gunfire, whooping Indians and the cavalry galloping to the rescue.

She'd slept on, right through the interval.

Hugh Blake's posthumous daughter had been the subject of a great many conversations in the weeks since her birth, and Emily, sipping her Coca Cola in a corner of the foyer, rocked her gently while chatting to various people who just had to have a peep at her.

Arriving back at their seats for the main film, Emily moved the baby to her other arm in an effort to ease the painful cramp in her shoulder, her discomfort catching Ryan's eye.

"Here Emily. Let me take her. She's too heavy for you to hold all night."

Startled, Emily stared up at him. She had no doubts her baby would be safe with him; he often claimed a cuddle when he came in from the paddocks, but his willingness to be seen assuming an almost parental role in public had surprised her.

She hesitated, debating in her mind whether or not she should accept his offer, when she felt another stabbing pain across her shoulders.

"Well, if you're sure, Ryan. I really would appreciate it. She's only a tiny mite, but she weighs heavy after a time."

"I wouldn't have offered if I wasn't," he retorted, reaching to carefully gather the sleeping baby into his arms. "There's no need to make a martyr of yourself, Em."

She smiled mistily up at him as the lights dimmed, flexing her aching muscles with relief.

Anyone who doesn't know us would think we're a family, Ryan, Didi and I, she daydreamed, letting her arm rest against his in the narrow seats of the theatre.

Wouldn't it be wonderful if ... If Hugh was right?

Afraid of tempting fate, she reined in her dreams and concentrated on the film she'd come to see.

Later, sharing the darkness of the back seat of the Holden with Joan, she hummed the catchy tunes from *Carousel* while she fed Didi; Ryan at the wheel with Charlie riding shotgun.

*****

Saturday night at the movies soon became a regular event. One at which Susan and Andrew Brandon usually joined them. When, one evening, they arrived without their daughter, Simone, Susan laughed out loud at Emily's surprise.

"She's sleeping through the night, now, Em, so Mum volunteered to babysit and give us a few hours to ourselves. She and Dad came last night. It feels strange, but so lovely and free to be just the two of us again." She didn't say another word, but, catching Joan's eye, raised her brow, tacitly hinting that maybe a similar arrangement could be introduced at *Emu Downs*.

The lights dimmed just then and the conversation was over. However, as the next weekend approached, Joan introduced the topic at dinner on Friday night.

"Charlie and I won't be going to town tomorrow night," she stated. "It's just that new American singer, Elvis Presley. He's not our cup of tea."

"Oh." Disappointed, Emily took a small bite of her steak and chewed it slowly. Elvis Presley may not have been Joan's cup of tea, but with his show-stopping good looks and melting, intimate voice, he was very much hers.

Love Me Tender was being touted in the magazines as the beginning of a new era in entertainment. The era of Rock and Roll.

"You'd like to go, though, wouldn't you Emily?" Ryan, who often found himself paying very close attention to her, hadn't missed her small, unhappy sound. He looked from Joan to Charlie, then back to Emily, sitting with her hands clasped in her lap, her eyes shining as she nodded her agreement.

"I'll take you. The Brandons will be sure to be there. I can't see Sue missing out on something that's all the rage. You two can get your heads together and have a good natter."

"Ryan, that'll be super!" It was all Emily could do not to throw her arms around him, she was so happy. Elvis and Ryan. She couldn't wait till Saturday. When Joan offered to mind Didi, she did give in to her emotions, wrapping her arms around the older woman in an enthusiastic bearhug.

'You're so good to me, Joan. Thank-you, thank-you, thank-you."

"Just be sure you're not too late getting home," Joan sniffed, trying not to let on how much Emily's gesture had touched her.

"Just think," Charlie chuckled, easing the drama, "We'll have our little princess all to ourselves." He rubbed his hands gleefully.

On Saturday, Emily hugged herself and gave a gurgling laugh.

"I know what Sue meant, about feeling free going out without her baby. Although, you know, Ryan? It feels really weird at the same time. As though something important is missing."

"You needn't worry about Didi, Em. Joan and Charlie will spoil her to bits. I reckon they've been scheming to get her to themselves for a while."

"I'm not worried. I know she'll be safe and well cared for. And Ryan. Thank you for driving me. I could have taken myself, but I think I'd have been nervous driving home alone, late at night."

"No thanks needed, Em." Ryan suddenly sounded gruff. "I enjoy your company. Reckon I might even enjoy this Elvis all you girls are so het up about."

"You will, Ryan. I promise you, you will. He's got a lovely voice."

When, by a happy coincidence, an Elvis song began playing on the radio, Emily sang along with him, her lilting soprano bringing a smile to Ryan's face. Emily even noticed him tapping the steering wheel in time to the music.

The evening was everything Emily could have wished for. Ryan was as attentive as if this was a real date, not just him doing her a favour, and Elvis lived up to her expectations. It wasn't until she paid a visit to the powder room before heading home that a sour note intruded.

Locked in the privacy of her cubicle, she couldn't help overhearing the conversations of other women availing themselves of the facilities.

"Did you see that young Madam flaunting herself for all the world to see?" Emily recognised the less than dulcet tones of Irene Smythe, and, wrinkling her nose, decided to wait till the coast was clear before emerging.

"Decked out in gaudy colours and hanging off young Farrelly's arm, and her supposed to be mourning that good man she tricked into marrying her," Mrs Smythe continued nastily.

She's talking about me! The horrid old cat!

Emily swallowed her gasp and resisted the temptation to burst out and confront her detractor.

"Oh, I don't know, Irene. I think you're being a bit harsh. Hugh always seemed very happy whenever I saw him. I doubt there was any trickery involved."

Emily distinctly heard Irene Smythe's disparaging sniff.

"He wouldn't have wanted a young thing like her to mope around in widow's weeds. The floral blouse she's wearing strikes a happy median, teamed with her dark green skirt." It had taken Emily a while to place her supporter as Mrs Partridge, the doctor's wife.

"Surely you're not denying it's unseemly of her to be here with a man, though, are you Elaine?"

"Well as far as that goes, he seemed more interested in talking to Andrew Brandon than Emily, you know, Irene. He probably just drove her in tonight as a friendly favour."

True, thought Emily. It was nice of Mrs Partridge to defend her, still, her spirits were rather cast down to hear her placidly stated observation.

"Although," Elaine Partridge continued, "It'd be a good match for both of them if they were to get together."

"We'll be seeing about that. Very soon." A triumphant note entered Irene Smythe's voice.

"Dear Vivienne will be home any day now. She and Ryan Farrelly are a couple, and I can't see her taking too kindly to Emily Blake muscling in on her territory. Especially now *Emu Downs* makes him a suitable match for her."

Another observation Emily would rather not have overheard.

The outer door squeaked opened and shut with a thud behind the two women as they left, cutting off any further eavesdropping.

Vivienne Dalgleish Emily's heart sank into her shoes. She'd hoped she'd seen the last of her. *Although I'm glad for him that English toff she went chasing off to England after escaped her clutches.* It might be mean of her, but she really, really disliked what she'd seen of Vivienne Dalgleish, and hoped Ryan wouldn't be fool enough to get tangled up with her again.

Reunited with Ryan for the drive home, Emily blamed her subdued mood on tiredness. Her pleasure in the night out sadly dimmed, she pretended to doze off in the corner of the front seat. It wasn't all pretence, though, as it seemed only moments later when the Holden rattled over the cattle grid, startling her awake.

EMILY'S BABY

15

Hearing the strident howls of an unhappy baby the minute they stepped out of the car, Emily cut short her thanks to Ryan and rushed inside to rescue her child.

"Didi, darling," she soothed, taking the baby from Charlie's arms. "What an awful racket to make when Nanna and Poppa Duffy are being so kind to you."

"She's only just started crying," Joan, defensive hackles so high they were almost visible, assured her. "She woke up a few minutes ago. Won't accept the bottle I offered her."

"I can see she's only just got started," Emily agreed. "Not a tear in sight. You're all noise, aren't you love? Are you hungry, then?" See gave a little laugh as the baby began tugging at the front of her blouse. "Thank you both so much. Now, I'd better do something about this starving morsel. Goodnight."

She hurried off to the nursery, passing Ryan in the lounge as she crossed it enroute to the bedroom wing.

"Goodnight Ryan," she called softly. "I had such a good time tonight."

EMILY'S BABY

When Emily and Joan arrived home from church the next morning, it was to an empty house, an explanatory note under the sugar bowl on the kitchen table fluttering in the breeze wafting in through the back door.

Fences down, and a mob of sheep out on the road.

Ryan.

"Oh dear," Joan muttered. "I suppose Charlie had to go with Ryan as the men have gone away for the weekend."

"I wonder when they'll be back? Just let me put this little one down in her cot and I'll help you with lunch, Joan."

Sunday lunch came and went with no sign of the men.

The dinner hour approached. Joan reheated the barely touched roast leg of lamb and the dishes of crisp roast vegetables and gravy she had prepared for Sunday lunch and still the absentees hadn't reappeared

"What'll I do with all this?"

Joan swept her hand wide, indicating the laden table.

"I can't abide waste!"

Surprised, Emily stared at the older woman.

It wasn't like Joan to get upset over things that were unavoidable. Looking closely, she saw new, deeply incised lines pulling her mouth down at the corners.

"Tell you what, Joan. You look bone-weary. Why don't you have an early night? I have to wait up till after Didi's late feed anyway, so I'll clear up. If the men get back before I turn in, I'll heat some of this lamb for them. And you know, Joan, I can't abide waste either, so I'll turn the vegetables into bubble and squeak for tonight, or for breakfast tomorrow. Either way, they won't go to waste."

It was a measure of just how tired Joan was, that she allowed Emily to shoo her out of the kitchen without protest. Staring after her, Emily couldn't help wondering if Joan's weariness had a deeper cause than being up late with Didi the evening before.

She'd been talking about retiring even before I came, she thought, *and then she had all that extra work with Hugh's illness and the nurses to cook and clean for. And now Didi.*

She wondered how old Joan Duffy actually was. Wondered, too, if the wiry little woman was really as strong and healthy as she claimed to be. All of a sudden she felt awfully selfish for taking her housekeeper for granted.

Grimacing guiltily, Emily vowed to take on even more of the household tasks than she had already claimed responsibility for. *The trick with that will be persuading Joan to ease up a bit.*

It was an hour later when the men finally trudged up the back steps to stick their heads around the kitchen door.

"We're starving, Em. Any chance of a bite to eat?" Charlie asked. He looked around, a worried frown creasing his brow. "No Joan?" he half-whispered.

"She was worn out, Charlie, so I sent her off to bed early," Emily answered.

"Now, if you two," she looked past Charlie to include Ryan in her command, "go and get cleaned up, I'll have a hot meal on the table for you by the time you get back."

"Already gone, Emily. Be generous with the portions, won't you?" Ryan led the way out, Charlie hanging back to ask one last question.

"Joan's okay, isn't she Em? Just a bit tired, like?"

"I think so, Charlie."

She may have reassured Charlie, but the fact he'd been worried gave her more food for thought.

*****

Laying a sleeping Didi down in her cot after the late feed, Emily was about to turn in for the night when she caught a whiff of cigarette smoke from the front veranda.

If Ryan is still up, she decided, *I'll just catch him for a quick word.*

She found him leaning against the veranda rail, half-smoked cigarette in one hand and a glass of scotch, ice-cubes tinkling melodically, in the other. Resting both elbows on the rail, she stood beside Ryan, gazing out over the paddocks.

"Thought you'd be in bed by now, Em."

"Soon." It was tempting to put the conversation she'd come out to have off till another day. Tempting, but cowardly. Emily gathered her courage and plunged in.

"Ryan, I'm a bit worried Joan's been overdoing things the last few months."

Her serious tone caught Ryan's attention. A crease formed between his eyes. Had he missed something important?

"I was thinking tonight, while I waited for you and Charlie to get back, that maybe I should make a move. Then she and Charlie can retire to their house in town."

"Hang on a minute, Emily. You don't want to go rushing into an important decision like that. I thought you liked it out here?"

"I do. This isn't about me, Ryan. It's about what's best for Joan; and you know she won't go if I'm still here, because of the gossip."

Ryan's frown deepened, the darkness hiding his suddenly bleak expression. She was right about Joan, only … He didn't want Emily to leave. Ever. He'd been attracted to her from the first moment he'd set eyes on her, but she'd been out of bounds. Now she wasn't, and he'd been warming to the idea planted in his mind by Hugh's letter hinting at the possibility of a future shared with Emily and her baby.

If she moved out, God only knew whether he'd ever have the chance to try his luck. It looked as if his time was about run out.

He crushed the stub of his cigarette in the ashtray at his elbow. Swallowing the last mouthful of what had become Dutch courage, he put the glass on the table nearby and clasped both hands loosely around Emily's upper arms, drawing her close.

"There's a perfectly acceptable way for Joan to retire if she wants to, and for you to stay here with me. If you want to?"

Emily stared at him, dumbfounded. Did he really mean what she thought? His declaration, out of the blue like that, had taken her completely by surprise.

"I ... I ... I don't know what to say."

And she really didn't.

It sounded as if Ryan was offering her her heart's desire, but was he? He'd not spoken one word of love. Or even marriage, really, except as a vague hint.

Before Emily could say another word, Ryan slid his arms right round her, pulling her up against his warm, firmly-muscled body. Not sure what to do with her hands, Emily placed them gingerly on his shoulders. She could feel him, hard as a rock, pressing against her belly. Pulse racing, excited, and yet almost afraid at the same time, she held her breath. Waiting.

Ryan lowered his head, slowly, giving Emily time to protest.

If she wanted to.

Mesmerised, Emily watched Ryan's chiselled lips lowering to hers. At the last moment, releasing her pent-up breath on a gasp, she rose on tip-toes. And closed the gap.

Expecting the hard, crushing kisses Luke had subjected her to, Ryan's soft, almost playful exploration of her mouth came as a wonderful surprise. Luke's kiss had repelled her. Ryan's, she couldn't get enough of. Tentatively, she kissed him back, mimicking the stroking of his tongue across her lips. Almost of their own accord, her lips parted for him and his tongue continued its explorations inside her mouth, finally mating with her tongue, seducing her into joining its dance.

Emily tasted the mingled flavours of tobacco and good scotch, and, stronger than both, the hot, spicy flavour of the man himself. The kisses deepened, becoming dizzyingly intense. She'd never imagined a kiss could consume her as Ryan's did.

When he lifted his head, she pulled him back to her, hungry for more.

Then she felt his hands on her breasts, kneading them, and fumbling at the buttons on her blouse.

"God, Emily. You're driving me insane. Let me touch you."

An alarm sounded through the passion fogging Emily's brain.

The words were different. Ryan begged, where Luke had demanded; but they both wanted the same thing from her. Something Emily wasn't ready to give.

Her hands, fisted in Ryan's shirt, released their grip. Flattening them against his chest, she pushed. Hard. It surprised her when he immediately stepped back, loosening his hold on her.

"S ... Stop," she whispered. Then, her pleading voice stronger, "No Ryan. Please stop."

Breathing heavily, Ryan turned aside. Releasing her entirely, he leaned propped himself up with both hands fisted on the veranda rail, his head turned away.

As his breathing eased, her turned his head to face her where she stood, rooted to the spot, her hands working nervously at her waist.

Damn it all! Ryan cursed silently. *How could I have misread the situation so bloody badly?*

Here he was, working himself up to a proposal, and the girl couldn't even stand to have him kiss her! His mind tried to tell him she'd been willing, more than willing even, until he'd gone too far, but he studiously ignored it.

She didn't want him; and that was that. He wouldn't be humiliating himself with her again. Perhaps she should leave, in which case, the sooner the better.

"I'm sorry, Emily. I shouldn't have kissed you. It won't happen again."

He turned from her, moving towards the side of the house where his rooms lay.

Mouth agape, Emily stared at Ryan.

Luke had ignored her when she begged him to stop. Ryan had obeyed her. Instantly. Even though it looked to her it hadn't been easy. Was this one of the differences between a good man and a scoundrel? It confirmed the belief she'd held since Hugh had first introduced him to her.

Ryan Farrelly was a good man. Who was about to slip through her fingers because she was too silly to tell the difference. Afraid this might be her one and only chance, she reached out, snagging the sleeve of his shirt with her fingers.

It took her till he halted, frowning eyes narrowed to slits staring over his shoulder at her, to form the words she needed to say.

"I'm glad you stopped when I asked you, Ryan, but I'm not sorry you kissed me." She needed a moment to recruit her courage to continue.

"I liked it. A lot. I kissed you back, remember?"

His expression lightening, Ryan relaxed. Gently disengaging the hand clutching his shirt, he kept it cradled within his large, capable ones.

"It was just, ... You went too fast, Ryan. I didn't know what to do. You see, I haven't had much experience with men."

Ryan stared hard at Emily, trying to read between the lines.

"But, you were married, Emily. Surely Hugh ..."

Emily shook her head, cutting in before he could finish his question.

"Hugh was dying, Ryan. He was totally honest with me, about that and everything else. We didn't have that kind of relationship." Her cheeks burned with a fiery blush she hopped the moonlight was too pallid to expose.

"He didn't really want a wife," Emily plugged doggedly on with the explanation now she'd started. "... but there was the baby, you see. What Hugh really wanted was the daughter he never had. Someone who would love him and care for him during his last months." This time she held Ryan's gaze for the longest time, willing him to understand.

"I was the best daughter I knew how to be. The best daughter he could ever have wished for."

"I ... see."

Ryan turned this surprising revelation over in his mind, discovering implausible discrepancies in her story. What kind of man got a girl he thought of as a daughter pregnant? Not the man he'd always considered Hugh Blake to be, that was for sure.

"You know, Emily," he said, choosing his words carefully, "I never really understood how the two of you met? You and Hugh? I don't actually know much about you at all. Family, stuff like that," he concluded.

All at once Emily's mind took her back to that awful, frightening night at The Gap.

Shaking her head, she refused to go there. Ryan didn't need to know the terrible despair which had drawn the two of them together.

Her family? Yes, she could face those memories.

"Last year was the most cataclysmic year of my life, Ryan. It started on New Year's Eve."

She wrapped her arms around her waist, her eyes looking unseeingly down at her feet. "Mum and Dad went to a party with friends from work. I was babysitting for neighbours. I'd just finished school, and had been accepted to train as a teacher, so I was earning every penny I could to help pay my way through college."

She'd diverged a little to give herself time to face what came next.

"There was an accident, and Mum and Dad were killed." A quaver in her voice, and a tear trickling down her cheek, betrayed her grief, and she hurried on recounting her story.

"The next weeks were absolutely dreadful. I went to college, but I was so deeply unhappy I didn't fit in very well with the other girls. Then ..." She was about to say 'Then I met Luke.' But decided against it.

"Everything went wrong. Those weeks at college were the most miserable of my life. I met Hugh by accident. He came to my rescue just when I thought I couldn't take any more. We liked each other right from the first. When he suggested we get married, I was happy to agree."

"I understand your becoming friends, but I don't see what Hugh had to offer a young girl like you. Aside from his money, that is."

Affronted, Emily straightened her back and tossed her head back.

"The money had nothing to do with it, except that having money is better than not having any. You want to know what I got out of my marriage, Ryan Farrelly? I got Didi. Without Hugh, I never would have had her."

It's the truth, even if it gives him entirely the wrong idea. Without Hugh I would have lost her. She'd have been taken from me and given to some childless couple to adopt.

"You told me you didn't have that kind of relationship with Hugh," Ryan said, groping to understand the implications of Emily's conflicting statements, "so who is Didi's father, Emily? Or was that all bunkum? Were you just trying to pull the wool over my eyes?"

Angry at what she thought he was accusing her of, Emily almost spat her words at him.

"Hugh Blake never touched me, but he is the only father Didi needs to know about."

Ryan still had questions, but Emily flung her hands up and backed away.

"I've had enough, Ryan. I can't take this inquisition any longer. I'm going in."

Suiting actions to words, she run inside, shutting the door behind her with a slam.

EMILY'S BABY

Left on his own on the veranda, Ryan ran his fingers through his hair, attempting to sort out the facts. If Hugh had never touched her, then that meant...? Some other bastard did, that's what it meant! It made him feel sick to his stomach to think of some rotter taking advantage of the grief-stricken young girl Emily had been. A rotter from whom Hugh had rescued her? He couldn't be sure, of course, but from her words tonight, that's what it added up to.

16

When Ryan appeared at the table for morning tea the next day, dressed for town in a jacket and tie, Joan looked him up and down suspiciously.

"Bit fancy for dagging sheep, aren't you?" she inquired, tittering at her own little joke; dagging being one of the dirtiest, least popular jobs on a farm.

"Mike and the others can handle the sheep," he replied. "Especially since it's not my favourite job by half. No Joan, fact is, the tractor's broken down again. They're predicting rain next week, so we need to finish planting if we're to have any chance of a decent winter crop this year. I'm on the way to town for replacement parts, then I've got an appointment with Harry Emden before lunch to see if he'll release the funds to buy the new tractor we desperately need; even though the estate's not through probate yet."

"If he won't, Ryan, I can lend you what you need."

Blushing, Emily offered him a second option. "That way you'll avoid hefty interest payments if you have to borrow."

Surprised, Ryan stared at Emily. How was she in the position to make such an offer? The tractor he wanted cost more than a new car.

"That's generous of you, Em, but it shouldn't be necessary."

"Are you sure you can afford that much, Emily?" Joan voiced the question Ryan had wanted to ask but had felt would be too impolite.

An even rosier blush spread across Emily's cheeks.

"When we married, Hugh transferred sufficient funds into my account to make me completely independent," she answered. "I've not touched a penny of it since." Shrugging, she dismissed the subject.

"Yes. Well, we'll see. Thanks, though, Em." Ryan shook his head. "Anyway Joan, I won't be back for lunch."

After taking Didi to wave 'Bye-bye' to Ryan, Emily put her on a rug on the grass in a sheltered corner, and settled down to help Charlie weed the garden.

She was just helping Joan wash the dishes after lunch when the phone rang. Wiping her hands on the kitchen towel, Emily hurried to the office to answer it.

"Em, how are you doing?"

"Sue! How lovely to hear from you. Everything's fine at my end. Better than fine, maybe," she added, thinking of her conversation with Ryan the night before.

And their kiss.

How she hoped he meant what he'd hinted at.

A chatty exchange followed, but nothing that couldn't wait till they saw each other at the CWA meeting on Thursday.

Emily was about to hang up when Sue abruptly came to the point.

"The reason I'm calling, Em. It's a bit embarrassing really. I don't approve of telling tales, only I suspect you're a lot fonder of Ryan Farrelly than you're letting on. If that's the case, I felt I ought to give you a heads-up on the word around town. Just in case someone springs it on you, catching you unawares."

"Why, Sue? Has something happened?"

"I'm not sure, Em, but here it is anyway. Vivienne Dalgleish is back."

"I knew she was expected."

"Well, she's here. I saw her myself, heading off to lunch with Ryan. Hanging onto his arm like a bloody clinging vine; both of them laughing and chatting as if they haven't got a care in the world."

"They did go out together quite a bit last year," Emily commented, her heart sinking to somewhere below ground level.

"That's not all, Em."

Susan sounded apologetic, but ploughed on anyway.

"Rumour, in the shape of Milly Roseworthy, who is usually reliable, is that earlier this morning Ryan was seen coming out of the jeweller's, mile-wide smile on his face, slipping a small package into his pocket. The grapevine's linking the two events, not that I believe for a moment it's true, mind."

Didi waking from her nap and demanding attention gave Emily the excuse she needed to terminate the call before Sue could begin speculating further.

Before she betrayed herself by bursting into tears.

Avoiding everyone for the next hour, she got her emotions under control. If Sue's rumours proved true, she'd have nothing to stay on *Emu Downs* for, and, feeling as she did about Ryan, the other side of Australia might be too close.

Maybe I really should be making plans to leave.

*****

Later that afternoon, the rattle of the cattle grid announced a visitor, just as Emily and the Duffy's were about to sit down to afternoon tea. Ryan had returned a short time earlier, grabbed a couple of freshly-baked scones, and headed straight out to the shed to work on the tractor, so they knew it wasn't him.

"Good thing I popped a batch of scones in the oven after lunch," Joan muttered. "Wonder who it is. They've got good timing, whoever they are," she grumbled, reaching for another place setting from the china cabinet.

Walking in, Didi balanced on her hip, Emily changed direction, going to the front door to welcome the visitors in. She just hoped it wasn't Sue following up on her phone call.

It wasn't. Instead, it was the person she least wanted to see.

Vivienne Dalgleish.

"Heard she was back," Joan muttered sourly looking over Emily's shoulder. "What's she want? Nothing good, I'll warrant."

"Maybe she's come to offer her condolences," Charlie, ever the peacemaker, offered. "Her and her mother were away for the funeral."

The three of them watched as Vivienne, dressed more suitably for the Ritz than the outback, elegantly extricated herself from the driver's seat of her father's pearl-grey Bentley. Straightening her skirt, she slammed the car door and picked her way up the path to the steps, carelessly leaving the garden gate open behind her.

"Still here, I see, Emily," she sneered, looking down on Emily from her superior height.

"I would have thought you'd have had the decency to take yourself off, back to whatever hole you crawled out from, long before now. Ryan calls you the mill-stone round his neck, you know." She sniggered. A nasty sound which, combined with her spiteful words, made Emily flinch. "He can't wait for you to pack your things and leave so he can finally have his house to himself."

Joan's horrified gasp at her back gave Emily the steel she needed to stand her ground. This horrid woman wasn't going to bully her. She bolstered her courage, reminding herself that Ryan hadn't acted as if he wanted her gone last night.

Quite the contrary. Although, her heart quailed momentarily, Sue's phone call did seem to support Vivienne's claim, at least in part.

Still uncowed, she opened her mouth to defend herself, but before she could utter a word, her opponent landed another, heavier, metaphorical body blow, driving the colour from her cheeks and the air from her lungs.

"See this?" Vivienne flourished her left hand under Emily's nose, causing the out-size diamond on her ring finger to flash a brilliant rainbow of colours.

"This is an engagement ring. Ryan and I will be getting married as soon as we can organise the wedding. I want you out of my house before then. Ryan might be too polite to give you your marching orders, but I'm made of sterner stuff, so you needn't go whining to him. Get yourself packed up and out of here by the end of the week, Emily Blake, or I'll have you thrown out!"

Joan finally found her voice. Launching a heated verbal attack, she defended Emily who had temporarily lost the ability to defend herself.

"It's you who'd better get out of here, Miss High-and-Mighty. Our Emily has every right to live here as long as she likes. And I'll bet Ryan won't like hearing what you're up to, even if he is stupid enough to be taken in by you. You're a nasty piece of work, Vivienne Dalgleish."

Without warning, Vivienne lashed out, striking the housekeeper across the face.

Didi, terrified by the loud, angry shouting, screamed. Emily shushed her, moving back to keep the child out of danger, but she needn't have bothered. She was no longer the focus of Vivienne's rage.

"You!"

Her voice dripping with venom, Vivienne turned her attack on Joan, and Charlie who'd stepped in front of his wife, fists at the ready.

"You, Joan Duffy. You're fired! And that miserable excuse for a man who's always hiding behind your back."

Emily reached out, holding Charlie back from giving the woman the thumping she deserved.

"Don't, Charlie. She's not worth it," she murmured.

"All of you useless parasites, stand aside. I'm going to see what, if anything, in this house is worth keeping and what I'll throw out when I move in." Vivienne barged her way past Joan and Charlie, intent on gaining entry to the house.

But this was going too far.

Sure of her ground in this, if nowhere else in the horrifying events unfolding, Emily blocked the door. Gathering dignity about her like a protective cloak, she refused to lower herself to the level of a public brawl.

"This is my home," she firmly but calmly informed the intruder, although her legs trembled with the effort of holding her upright, "and the things in it all belong to me. You have no right to come here ordering us about. If you're not gone in the next few seconds, I'll call the police and have you charged with assaulting Joan."

"And if you don't hurry up and get down those steps, I'll be helping you down with my boot up your backside," Charlie, angrier than Emily had ever seen any man, came to stand should-to-shoulder with her.

Outnumbered and outfaced, Vivienne scuttled back to the car.

"Oh, and Vivienne?"

Emily fired her parting shot.

"You're not welcome in this house. As long as I live here, you won't be invited to put one foot through the gate; engaged to Ryan or not!"

"You haven't heard the last of this, Emily Blake." Vivienne flung the words out the window of the car, accelerating viciously across the home paddock and across the cattle grid.

The silence she left in her wake was broken only by Didi's hiccupping sniffles. Emily rubbed her gently on the back, dropping a kiss on her blonde curls.

"It's okay, Baby. The wicked witch is gone," she murmured, not taking her eyes off the fading dust cloud heading towards the main road.

Gradually the tension shared by the three victors eased. Taking charge, Emily turned to her co-hort of staunch defenders, a wobbly smile on her face.

"She's gone. I need to sit down before I fall down on the spot. My legs feel like jelly."

"Kettle's probably boiling its head off in there. I'll make the tea" a very subdued Joan offered. "I'm sure we can all do with a cup."

"Sure can, Joanie love. You all right? It was quite a wallop she gave you. That spoiled madam oughta have had her backside tanned a time or two to teach her some manners." He stroked his wife's cheek where the imprint of Vivienne's hand still showed.

"What the bloody Hell's our Ryan doing, getting himself tangled up with the likes of her?"

"Maybe he's in love with her," Emily suggested, her voice a bleak travesty of her normal cheerful tones. Ignoring Joan's huff of disbelief, she added, "Or maybe he's ambitious enough to want to add *Balmoral* to *Emu Downs* by marrying Brad Dalgleish's daughter."

One of those reasons had to be the truth. There was simply no other explanation any of them could think of.

"Anyway, Charlie, if you'll shut the gate behind her, I think Joan's cuppa is a fine idea. Come on, Didi. Let's find you a nice bikkie."

A suggestion the baby thought even finer.

*****

Cuppa over, Emily, who had been unusually quiet throughout, wiped the biscuit smears from her daughter's face and lifted her out of the high-chair. Instead of abating, the flames of her anger had burned steadily higher. Anger with Vivienne, but also with Ryan. How dare he lead her on, implying an interest which it now seemed had been utterly false? Bent on revenge, she set off for the office to phone Harry Emden.

"Mrs Blake, how lovely to hear from you," the lawyer said, sounding quite jovial. "If it's the new tractor you're ringing about, it's all sorted, my dear. Can't see any reason not to advance the money to Ryan."

"Actually, Mr Emden, that's not why I'm calling. There was one of the clauses of Hugh's will I'd like you to explain to me. With Didi making herself felt at the time, I didn't pay as much attention as I ought to have done."

"And how is the little dear? It's not every day there's a baby delivered practically in my chambers. Feel I've got a vested interest, you know."

"Didi's thriving, Mr Emden. The thing I'm not sure of is, when Hugh said the homestead was mine till I left *Emu Downs,* did he mean just the one year he wanted me to stay for, or did he mean it was mine forever, if I chose to make my home here permanently?"

"Just let me look the will over again, my dear, while I check the exact wording. I wouldn't want to give you the wrong advice."

When he got back to Emily a few minutes later, she listened carefully as he read the relevant clause to her, a rather grim smile forming. She hadn't been mistaken. She'd read her copy of the will very carefully, and Harry Emden confirmed her understanding of the exact wording Hugh had used.

"Thank you so much, Mr Emden. I know how careful one has to be in legal matters."

"Not at all, Mrs Blake. Glad to be of service."

17

"Thank goodness for Mick Jones. He was a good recommendation of yours, Charlie. With his mechanical know-how we've got the old tractor running again."

Ryan, slicked-back hair still damp from the shower, hurried to take his place as the household were about to sit down to dinner.

"Yeah. He's a decent bloke, Mick Jones. Reliable," Charlie responded woodenly, carefully not looking at Ryan when he spoke. "Good to know he's working out okay."

"Better than okay, Charlie. I'll let him take over the planting, and nurse the old girl along. Hopefully the new one will be delivered before she conks out again. Harry Emden came through with the money, so I buzzed down to McLean's and ordered the new one immediately."

This time a grunt was all the response Ryan got from Charlie. In the flurry of settling into chairs and passing the serving dishes and meat platter around, he didn't notice he'd been ignored by both women.

"Hello, Chickie," Turning to greet the baby whom Emily had tucked into the high chair positioned between herself and him, he tickled Didi under the chin, making her laugh and slap her hands on the tray.

"Didi!" Emily's voice was unwontedly sharp as she urged her daughter to sample a little of the mashed vegetables and gravy she'd prepared for her.

A frown flitted across Ryan's face. He looked at Emily, concerned by the pinched look to her face.

"Are you okay, Em?"

"Nothing the matter with me," she muttered, keeping her eyes on the food she was spooning into Didi's mouth.

"You seem to be in top form this evening."

Joan's comment drew his attention away from Emily, mainly because her caustic tone was so rarely directed towards him. He sat up, looking quickly at his dinner companions, none of whom appeared to be their usual cheerful selves. There was none of the usual lively chatter, exchanging news and views. Now he thought of it, his announcement about the new tractor hadn't elicited the interest he'd expected, either.

Something was going on here. Something Ryan didn't like. A bad feeling which he felt was directed at him, permeated the room.

This wasn't the happy group he'd had morning tea with this morning.

"You all look put out with me about something," he said, determined to get to the bottom of it. "What is it I've done? Or not done?"

No-one spoke for a moment A long moment, during which the Duffy's actually squirmed uncomfortably in their chairs. Ryan was about to ask again, when Emily set Didi's spoon down with exaggerated care and looked up, facing him fully for the first time since he'd entered the room. Her defiant expression shocked him to the core.

"We had an unexpected visitor this afternoon. She left us all feeling rather upset. Joan especially, when she hit her across the face, nearly knocking her down."

Ryan's eyes flew to Joan's face, easily discerning the bruise darkening her right cheek.

"What the ...?" About to use language unsuitable for the dinner table, he pulled himself up and started again.

"Who? I can't imagine anyone we know doing such a thing!"

"Your bloody bitch of a fiancée, that's who!" Charlie, whose temper had also been simmering all afternoon, wasn't so particular in his choice of words. All his anger and frustration burst out, aimed at the only available target – Ryan Farrelly.

Flabbergasted, Ryan stared at him, mouth agape.

"Why couldn't you trust us with the news yourself, Ryan?" Joan was near tears, her voice no longer robust, but an old woman's pitiful quaver. "We've always treated you like a son, and you do this to us?"

"Do what to you? What fiancée? Who are you talking about?"

A sinking feeling in his gut told Ryan he already knew the answer, but he asked anyway.

"As Charlie said," it was Emily who answered, her clipped diction and English accent, more pronounced than usual, proclaiming her disdain.

"Your fiancée. Vivienne Dalgleish," she elaborated, her short, straight nose elevated as if in avoidance of a nasty smell.

"She arrived on the doorstep this afternoon, flashing your engagement ring and throwing her weight around. After ordering us to vacate the premises by week's end, she went on to tell Joan and Charlie, in extremely unpleasant terms, they were fired," Emily, having assumed the mantle of spokesperson, elucidated; so clearly there was no misunderstanding her words.

"When Joan told her off, she hit her across the face. I had to resort to threatening to call the police to make her leave. I'm sorry if it upsets you to hear this about the woman you're planning to marry, and quite soon, according to her, but she behaved like a madwoman. She sounded utterly deranged."

"Completely off her trolley," Charlie corroborated.

"Why you had to take up with a nasty piece like her, I don't know," Joan sniffed.

"You could have done ever so much better for yourself."

Ryan's mouth had compressed into a tight, white line, his fists clenched on the tablecloth.

It was even worse than their first words had led him to fear. And he hadn't heard it all yet. Emily began speaking again before he could answer their accusations.

"If you had been courteous enough to tell us yourself that you were engaged, we'd all have wished you happy."

Out of sight below the tablecloth, Emily crossed her fingers against the lie.

"Even though we can't see how anyone married to *her* could ever be happy. I would have begun making plans to let you have the house, but now I'm so angry I've decided I'm not going anywhere." Running short of breath, Emily's tirade slowed to a halt, but, gasping in a shuddering breath, she continued, not waiting for a response.

"You need to straighten her out on a few facts, though, Ryan. She seemed to be under the impression this is your house. It is not! Not until such time as I choose to leave it. Until then, it is mine; and its contents, down to the last tattered cleaning rag, remain mine, whatever I choose to do. I checked with Mr Emden after she left, to make sure *I* had *my* facts straight. Vivienne Dalgleish is never setting foot in Hugh Blake's house. It's not what he would have wanted. You'll have to build her a new one, or, better still, move in with her at *Balmoral*."

The ticking of the grandfather clock in the next room sounded loud in the silence when Emily finished saying her piece. She'd said more than she'd meant to, but she didn't regret a word. Not one single word. Ryan Farrelly had made his bed, as her mother used to say, and now he could lie in it. If he had any decency at all, he'd move out immediately. She hoped he would. She'd be glad if she never had to see him again; even though it would break her heart.

Ryan, nausea and temper fighting for supremacy, let his gaze circle coldly around the table, carefully studying each angry countenance staring in his direction. He crumpled his napkin and tossed it down beside his plate. Pushing his chair back, he rose to his feet, leashed fury blazing from his eyes.

"If you've all had your say?" He looked long and hard at each of them once more. "Because if you have, there are a few things I'd like to say. I thought I could count on you for friendship and support. I thought you, all of you," his eye settled on Emily, whose agonised gaze was fixed on his face, her hands working nervously in her lap, "knew me better than to believe this load of codswallop you've been spewing out."

"Steady on, there, Mate. She was flashing a ring. Said you gave it to her. And you were going out with her for months. We had no grounds not to believe her." Charlie laid his hand over his wife's, cautioning her to leave the talking to him.

"What Charlie says is not all, Ryan," Emily added. "I had other information from a source I trust, before she even arrived. You were seen at the jeweller's in town, then you and Vivienne, looking all lovey-dovey were seen going to lunch in the *Southern Cross*."

Ryan closed his eyes. Taking a deep breath, he fought to bring his temper under control. Vivienne had said she'd make him sorry, and she had. The three people he cared most about had been turned against him. If he was to have any hope of retrieving the situation, he couldn't afford to alienate them further. Shoving his fists in his pockets, he lifted his head and stared them down.

"You all know very well that I've never lied to you, any of you," his gaze sought Emily's once more. "I'm not going to start now, so listen carefully. I am not engaged. To anyone. I don't have a fiancée. I've not given anyone an engagement ring. Ever. And if I do choose to get engaged, it won't be to Vivienne Dalgleish. Charlie, you're right," this time his eyes sought out his old friend.

"I did go out with her for a while last year, but that was ended before she went off on her travels. I haven't set eyes on her for months, and far from wanting to take up with her again, I hope not to see her again. Ever. I took her to the *Southern Cross* to make my position clear to her away from public view as I had been warned she wasn't above making a spectacle of herself when she was crossed. She stormed off, and I hoped that was the end of it. Obviously, I was wrong." He turned to Joan, next.

"I'm more sorry than I can say, that you had to suffer such an indignity, Joan. You needn't fear a repeat, I'll see to that."

He looked down at his plate where his untouched meal was congealing in gravy that had gone cold.

"I've lost my appetite," he muttered. "I'll leave you to it."

Three heads turned as one, watching him stalk off in the direction of the office, then turned to face each other with identical painful, guilty expressions.

The ensuing silence was broken by Didi, who, tiring of the rusk Emily had handed her earlier, began banging with her spoon on the tray of the hIgh-chair.

"Seems we misjudged the boy."

"Maybe, Joanie, but how were we to know?" Charlie muttered, patting her hand consolingly.

Emily wiped moisture from her eyes with an unsteady hand. She'd sunk her chances of a future with Ryan, good and proper, that was for sure.

EMILY'S BABY

18

When Emily took Didi off to bath her and get her ready for bed, she looked for Ryan, but there was no sign of him. Not even the familiar aroma of cigarette smoke to point her in the right direction.

Her spirits sank even lower than they already were. She'd held a forlorn hope that if she apologised, he might forgive her. It seemed not even that small solace was to be granted tonight. After his vehement rejection of the woman, she didn't make the mistake of assuming he'd turned to Vivienne; but it seemed he wasn't looking for a reconciliation with herself, either.

Sighing drearily, she attended to Didi's small needs then, the baby tucked up for the night, filled the tub for herself, tossing in a handful of lavender bath crystals in the hope they'd help soothe her troubled mind.

An hour later she gave up tossing and turning in fruitless pursuit of sleep. Getting up, she pulled a silk kimono on over her broderie-anglaise nightie and went to check on her child who slept peacefully under her light blanket. Even Didi didn't want her tonight.

For want of anything better to do, Emily trailed off to the kitchen. Maybe a mug of warm cocoa would succeed where the lavender scented bath had failed.

"Is there enough for two?"

Almost dropping the spoon, Emily swung round, hand to her chest where her heart thudded heavily.

"Ryan!" she gasped. "You scared the life out of me. I didn't hear you come in."

The sight of his tall, well-muscled figure filling the doorway set her heart thudding just as rapidly, but in a new, happier, rhythm.

"Of course there's enough for two. I'll just add a spot more milk."

Gathering her courage, she turned to cast her eyes up to his face in an unconscious plea.

"I ... I'm s ... sorry, Ryan. I didn't want to believe Vivienne this afternoon, but after what I'd already been told, I didn't know what to think. Then she started abusing us all and my temper got the better of me. I'm so sorry."

Moving to stand by her side, Ryan reached out to take her unoccupied hand.

"Did last night mean so little to you that you'd believe that nonsense, even for a minute?"

He rubbed his thumb across her palm, the gentle caress distracting her. Rosy colour fluctuated wildly on her milky-fair skin. She looked at him, then quickly looked away again.

Ryan waited.

Sneaking another upward glance, Emily whispered,

"Our kiss meant a lot to me, Ryan, but I wasn't sure what it meant to you. You hinted at a future together, but you didn't commit yourself to anything. You see, in the past I was taken in by a smooth-talking man whose only interest was in satisfying his own selfish desires." She heard Ryan's sharp inhalation.

"I know you're not like *him*, Ryan." She hastened to assure him. She certainly didn't count him in that class of man. "But I don't have very much experience with men. The kiss was nice, but then everything started going so fast, I got scared. For a moment it almost felt like being back with *him*."

Ryan's grip on her hand tightened almost painfully. Realising from her attempt to release herself that he was hurting her, he loosened his grip while still holding her hand captive.

"That's the difference, though, Ryan." Emily looked down at the joined hands. "You'd let me go if I asked. Like last night, and just now. He didn't. He said we'd gone too far to stop, and blamed what happened on me."

Ryan felt her hand trembling within his. With one finger under her chin, he lifted Emily's downcast face. Tears filled her eyes, threatening to overflow and course down her pale cheeks.

"That's not true, Em," he whispered gently, suddenly afraid of inadvertently scaring her

"A man can always stop. If he doesn't, he's not worthy of being called a man. No woman should ever be forced like that, Emily. It's her right to say whether she wants his attentions or not."

"Damn!" The smell of hot milk caught Ryan's attention.

At Ryan's mild curse, Emily swung back to the stove, just as he reached past her to rescue the milk a split second before it boiled over. He poured it into the mugs standing ready on the table.

"Let's take these through to the lounge before we wake Joan up. It's a bit cool for the veranda tonight."

Obediently, Emily picked up her mug and followed him through the house. His words had echoed Hugh's when she'd told him her story, further reassuring her.

"Emily," Ryan was unusually hesitant, but persevered. "I don't know if it's too late to take action against that bloke for what he did to you, but I can find out. If you want me to, that is. I'd be a bit wary of landing you in the middle of something that could become deuced unpleasant unless it was what you wanted to do."

"Oh, Ryan, that's so good of you." Emily reached over to pat his hand lying on the arm of his chair.

"There's no need to do anything, though. Hugh used his influence to notify the people concerned that Luke was an inappropriate person to be teaching young women. He got his lawyer in Sydney to write it so the message would get to the right people with no come-back. The rotten louse got the sack soon after, when an investigation brought similar cases of misconduct to light. I wasn't the only one, you see. Not even the first. Now I just want to forget all about him, and most of the time I do."

They sat, sipping their hot drinks in silence, each processing the conversation from their particular viewpoint.

Ryan still felt the least he should do was give the bastard a good thrashing, but he could hardly go haring off to Sydney after him when he had no idea where to find him.

Much as it went against the grain, Emily was right. He'd best let it go or he'd risk making her the subject of particularly nasty gossip.

"Ryan?" Attentively, he lifted his face to Emily's. "What I said earlier?"

Ryan cast his mind back, trying to recall the conversation before Emily's startling disclosure.

"About this afternoon? I really am sorry for doubting you. Do you think you could … I mean, is it possible for you to, … to forgive me?"

The heart-breaking uncertainty in Emily's voice aroused every last protective instinct within Ryan which hadn't already been engaged by her story.

"Emily." He put his mug down on the table. Crouching in front of her, he cupped her face lightly between his palms.

"Em, there's nothing to forgive. I understand how it was for you today, dragged into a scene like that without warning. It's me who ought to be begging your forgiveness for losing my temper tonight and making it all worse. That was my intention when I accosted you in the kitchen, only we got sidetracked by other issues. Can you forgive me, dearest Emily?"

With no hesitation at all, Emily reached out to lay one small hand on Ryan's cheek. Her action said it all, but she confirmed it, repeating Ryan's own words back to him.

"There's nothing to forgive, Ryan. Nothing at all. I let my temper run away with me too, so I understand exactly what that's like." She smiled mistily at him, then added reflectively, "You know, Ryan? I didn't even know I had such a temper till I lost it with Vivienne. I don't think I like that part of me very much."

Ryan turned his head, placing a warm kiss in the palm of the hand still cradling his face, his action bringing a hot blush to Emily's cheeks.

"I like every part of you, Em. Even your temper."

Rising to his feet, he swung her up in his arms.

Emily squeaked, clutching at his shoulders for support. Then he was sitting on the sofa in the exact spot she had been a moment before, and she was on his lap, her arms wound around his neck, his lips on hers. And she was kissing him back as if her life depended on it, pouring every ounce of the love she felt for him into the kiss. Lost in a world of bliss, Emily was unaware of time passing. Aware only of the passionate inferno blazing between them. An inferno on the point of consuming them both.

Then Ryan was prising his mouth from hers, holding her at arms-length, frustrating her desire to continue the kiss. Disappointed to be cast down from the heaven she'd briefly been invited into, Emily groaned, pouting.

"Shush."

Breathing heavily, Ryan hushed her, tucking her head under his chin where she cuddled against his chest. "Gotta stop, Em. We're playing with fire, here."

She giggled, wriggling into a more comfortable position. She could feel his rock-hard arousal pressing against her; could feel the racing beat of his heart beneath her hand and the rasp of his breath before it settled to a regular rhythm.

Lying warm and safe, protected, in his embrace, she fiddled with the top button of his shirt, marvelling at the difference made by the identity of one's lover. Luke had revolted her after the first sweet kisses which had lulled her into a danger she couldn't escape. Ryan's kisses, on the other hand, left her yearning for more. She knew with Ryan she'd never fear his masculine desires. In fact, right this very minute, she wished he'd shown less restraint.

Seeking to control his baser urges, Ryan leaned his head back, holding Emily against his chest so he'd be less likely to give in to the temptation to kiss her again. *Who'd have thought*, he mused, *that when I stormed out of the dining room, I'd end up here tonight?*

"Know something, Em?" he murmured, still thinking of the strange quirks of fate. "What happened here this afternoon was probably all my fault."

Curious, Emily leaned back so she could study his face.

"How do you figure that?"

"Well, when I ran into her in town, Vivienne latched onto me, clinging to my arm like a confounded barnacle, waffling on about how happy she was to be home again, and how happy to be with me. When she started saying how much she'd missed me, and how wonderful it was that there was no longer any impediment to our marriage, I knew I was in for a rough time."

He felt Emily withdrawing herself from his arms and held her in place.

"Wait! Hold up there, Em, and hear me out. Vivienne had no cause to be talking of marriage. We'd never had that kind of relationship. We were both at a loose end last year and went out a few times on a strictly casual basis. She'd have been the first to think it a hilarious joke if I'd wanted more. Too low down on the social scale, and not enough in the bank. Then. Seems inheriting *Emu Downs* has elevated me to a higher rung. Charlie accused me of having my eye on *Balmoral*, when I made my peace with him and Joan a bit earlier, but it was all the other way round."

Emily's fist thumping into his ribs almost had him dumping her on the floor.

"Oww! What's that for, Em?"

"You went to see the Duffys but not me! That's what for."

"You were busy with Didi. I hung about, hoping you'd come back, but your lights went out and I figured I wouldn't get a chance to make my peace with you till tomorrow. Couldn't believe my luck when I saw you in the kitchen."

"Okay, then." Emily snuggled back down on his lap. "Go on, then. Finish the story."

"Right. Well. I couldn't face what was shaping up to be a nasty confrontation out in the middle of the street, so I hustled her into the back room of the *Southern Cross* and fetched her a drink. Then I told her how far off-beam she was. Reminded her there'd never been any talk of marriage in the past, and wasn't going to be, not now or in the future."

Ryan paused a moment, then decided not to hold back.

"I told her I'd found someone new while she was lording it up in England. She guessed I meant you, Em. She raged on a while longer, trying to use *Balmoral* and her father's money to outweigh your inheritance from Hugh, but I said it was you, the woman, not your money, I wanted. Big mistake. She flung her drink in my face and stormed off, shouting how she'd make me sorry. Well, I had nothing to hang around for, so I came straight back. She must have stewed over her grievances for a while, then, well … You know the rest, Em."

Emily had heard all he said, but there was really only one thing which interested her.

"Did you really mean it, Ryan?"

"Mean what Em?"

His obtuseness earned him another thump in the ribs.

"You know what. Do you really want me, Ryan? They way you told her? Me, not my inheritance?"

"I thought I'd already made that clear. I don't kiss a girl unless I mean it."

Emily wrinkled her nose, still looking unconvinced, and Ryan recalled her earlier comments. When he'd asked about last night, she'd answered that he'd not made any commitment, so she hadn't been sure what their kiss had meant to him. What *she* meant to him. Baring his soul went against the grain, but if that was what it took, he'd do it a hundred times over.

Emily was too important to him to leave the tiniest shred of doubt in her mind.

"You mean the world to me, Em. If you'll have me, I want to marry you. Young Didi is included in that, too. I want you both."

Emily smiled at him, but she didn't answer. Ryan felt she was waiting. What more did she expect from him? He'd told her he … No. He hadn't.

"I love you Emily, with all my heart. Will you marry me?"

Throwing her arms around his neck, Emily answered him with kisses. It was quite a while later that Ryan once again put space between them before he lost control.

"So, my dearest, darling Emily, what's your answer?"

"My answer?" Emily, dazed by heady kisses, suddenly looked confused.

"Oh," she said, her pout tempting him to kiss her rosy lips again. "I remember now."

She sat up, and speaking very clearly, gave him his answer.

"Ryan Farrelly, it will make me very, very happy to marry you, because I love you, too. I think I've loved you almost from the day we first met, only I wasn't free then. I am now."

"Then, I guess we need this."

Ryan reached into the side pocket of his cotton trousers, bringing out a small package from which he extracted a box covered in blue velvet.

"Ooh…" Emily's eyes widened, and seemed filled with stars as she watched Ryan remove a lovely diamond solitaire ring from the box. Watched him pick up her left hand, and, his voice a little husky, make her a solemn promise as he slid the ring onto the fourth finger.

"With this ring, I pledge myself to you, Emily, for as long as we both shall live."

"Oh, Ryan, I do love you. You're the only man I'll ever love. This is the most perfect ring I've ever seen." She moved her hand, and the ring emitted rainbow fire that sparked and flashed in the dimly lit room.

"It fits perfectly, too," Emily marvelled.

"You left your rings on the windowsill after washing up the other day. I borrowed one and drew around the inside. The woman in the jeweller's shop matched it for size."

"You're so clever, Darling."

Emily would have gone on, except that Ryan gave in to temptation and began kissing her all over again.

EMILY'S BABY

Epilogue

The CWA meeting that Thursday took quite a while to come to order. When Joan and Emily stepped through the door, it was to hear Mavis Dalgleish holding forth on the outstanding success of her dear Vivienne during their trip to England.

"... and really, Lord Egglington was quite smitten. If he'd had his way, I'd have returned to Australia alone. Only my daughter was so homesick, not even prospect of garden parties with Her Majesty in attendance could compensate her for never seeing her homeland again."

"Baloney! Bet Lord Whosits saw through her and dropped her like a hot potato."

Sue, immediately joining her friend, whispered behind her hand in Emily's ear.

"You know, I'm expecting the dear girl to share some exciting news with her father and I, any day now," Mavis blathered on. "Last year we discouraged her association with young Farrelly, but during our absence his prospects have improved substantially."

A contemplative expression on her face, Emily chose that moment to ostentatiously examine her engagement ring. Except for the Duffys she'd not shared her news with any of her friends yet, but she wasn't prepared to listen to Mavis Dalgleish a minute longer.

Ryan was *hers*, not Vivienne's.

"Emily!" Sue's shriek drew every eye to where the two girls sat, Sue now holding her friend's hand up to show off the ring.

"Is that what I think it is?"

Emily laughed; a trill of pure joy.

"I'm engaged, Sue. Ryan asked me to marry him, and I said yes."

Mavis abruptly sank into her chair, mouth pursed as if she'd sucked on a lemon.

"Huh. Opting for second best, I suppose. Darling Vivienne must have turned him down. I always thought that young man had an eye for the main chance."

Irene Smythe's words fell like damp squibs into the silence following Emily's announcement.

"Actually, Mrs Smythe," Barbara Elliot moved to stand behind her chair at the head of the table, "I rather think Emily is Ryan's first, last and only choice. He confided in me some time ago that he was waiting till a decent interval had passed before making his feelings known to her. I'm sure I speak for everybody here when I offer you my congratulations, Emily, dear."

A babble of voices called their congratulations as Barbara Elliot clapped her hands sharply to call the meeting to order.

Catching Emily's eye, she gave her a surreptitious wink. Ryan had confided nothing of the sort, but she wasn't above prevarication if she felt the situation warranted it.

"Before we get this meeting under way, ladies," Barbara continued, speaking in her most authoritative tone, "I have one more thing to say on the matter of Emily's engagement." She paused until the rustling and scraping of chairs stilled. "As we are all aware, the circumstances are somewhat unusual. However, I believe we can all agree that with the two parties living practically in each other's pockets, there is no need for a lengthy engagement, as long as the wedding is a relatively quiet, respectful affair."

Barbara Elliot didn't throw her not inconsiderable weight around often, her style being more inclined to subtle persuasion than outright coercion, but when she did, the ladies of St Denis listened.

*****

Assured they would meet with nothing but good-will, despite the shortened mourning period following Hugh Blake's death, Emily and Ryan, ably assisted by Joan, planned a simple wedding to be held on the first Saturday in July.

The ceremony, held at eleven o'clock in the morning, preceded a buffet luncheon at *The Southern Cross* hotel. Restricting the guest list to a mere thirty people meant only their very best friends were invited. On discovering they had been omitted, Mavis Dalgleish and her chief crony, Irene Smythe were heard to make disparaging comments on the shabbiness of the affair, but they were in the minority.

The pink dress she had worn for her wedding to Hugh had been a party dress; this time Emily was determined to appear a true bride.

Ryan's bride.

Clad in ballerina-length white silk trimmed with Chantilly lace, a short veil covering her long, blonde hair, Emily was a dream come to life as Ryan watched her approach him down the flower bedecked aisle on Charlie Duffy's arm. At the last minute before placing her hand in Ryan's, she turned to blow a kiss to her baby, sitting solemnly on Joan's lap in the front pew. Recognising her mother, Didi bounced up and down, holding her arms out to be picked up. However, Joan had come prepared, and the child's attention was easily diverted with a honey-baked rusk.

THE END

I hope you enjoyed reading

Emily's Baby.

Please turn the page for a preview of Lena West's next Australian Historical Romance,

Home is the Heart

Here is Your Preview of

Home is the Heart

An Australian Historical Romance

1

"Eliza! Eliza, I've 'eard the most amazin' news!"

So excited he forgot the careful enunciation he sometimes tried to copy from his wife, Jason Baker, wavy brown hair in its usual state of disarray, burst into their bedroom where Eliza, only just returned herself, sat waiting for him.

Just yesterday, along with a host of other new immigrants who had crossed the world on the same ship, they had travelled up the Swan River to Perth from the port of Freemantle where they had disembarked the day before.

Advised there would be more opportunities for both of them to find work in the larger town, they had settled into this migrant hostel in the interim.

It had been a shock to Eliza to find the city of Perth all new and raw compared to her old home in Manchester, but the people she had met were lovely; so friendly and helpful she felt buoyed up by optimism. Although she had failed to find work during the day, she had a list of other businesses to approach on the morrow.

"Have you found work, then, Jason? Already? How wonderful."

Eliza ran to her husband, clapping her hands in delight.

Thrilled to the core with his exciting news, Jason lifted Eliza off her feet, twirling her round and round till, laughing and beginning to feel giddy, she begged him to set her back on her feet. A bit unsteady, she clung to him, gazing adoringly, trustingly, into his beloved face.

"Not work, my love. Even better. You'll never guess, Eliza."

He wrapped his arms around his lovely young wife, seizing the opportunity to steal a kiss.

"Jason, whatever do you mean?" Emerging from her husband's kiss, Eliza pushed back to look into his face, alive and glowing with excitement as she'd never seen it before. Infected by his enthusiasm, a corresponding excitement began to fizz in her veins. She sank back onto the bed where she had been sitting, tugging Jason down beside her.

"Tell me quickly, Jason. What could possibly be better than finding a good job on your first day of looking? What's got you all het up?"

One hand holding Eliza's, Jason leaned forward, eager to share his news.

"It's gold, darlin'," he whispered, voice lowered so no-one passing by outside could overhear.

"Gold! Just think on it, Eliza." He said, eyes glowing.

"They're diggin' gold outta the ground at a place called Southern Cross. It's there fer the takin' fer anyone who's prepared to search fer it. All yer need is a licence and then yer can pick yer spot and stake a claim."

A disquieting chill feathered down Eliza's spine.

"Where did you hear this, Jason? Are you sure you've got it right?"

"What if we go haring off to this Southern Cross place and find the gold is all run out? Or the good claims have all been taken?"

Eliza thought for a moment. Jason was a good man, the best, but she didn't trust this talk of gold. Didn't believe their fortune could be made so easily.

"I've been askin' around."

Jason grinned. He knew his Eliza. Pretty as a picture with her trim figure, yellow ringlets and trusting blue eyes, she'd captured his heart the moment he'd set eyes on her. He liked the way she kept him on an even keel, considering her cautious nature the perfect foil to his own impetuosity. This time though, his eyes blinded by gold-lust, he set about convincing her this new dream was at least a possibility.

"Seems the first gold was discovered in 1887. Only a few months ago, Eliza. Round about the time we were gettin' ourselves married last year, but they're only now startin' to get organised. If we go right away Lizzie darlin', we'll be in at the start, afore the big companies start buyin' the little miners up. I met up wiv an old chap called George Sampson. He's been chasin' gold from California to New South Wales and now 'ere."

"He knows what to look fer. I'll take yer ta meet him tomorra and yer can hear it fer yerself. He's promised to tell us 'ow to go about it if we're interested. He's found several fortunes, 'e said, and lost 'em all through foolishness. This time he's planin' to set 'imself up for 'is old age. Reckons if we 'ave a go and do well, we'll be set up fer life. If we don't, then we come back 'ere and look for work as we originally planned. Either way, we won't lose out, and we might just end up rich. All fer a bit o' hard work. We can do it, Lizzie. We can an' all."

Eliza nodded her head, glad to see Jason hadn't quite lost all touch with reality. She had been staring open mouthed, looking up at him as he talked, listening and taking it all in. She loved him so much, this strong, energetic young man who had swept her off her feet, persuading her to marry him and emigrate with him to Western Australia.

Initially, Eliza hadn't really wanted to leave England. Australia had seemed so frighteningly alien and far away. Finally, with the onset of a miserable English winter, the promise of sunshine and blue skies had won her over. Now, the idea of Jason's proposed treasure hunt churning in her brain, she gazed expectantly into his eager brown eyes.

Jason Baker couldn't really be termed handsome, she thought indulgently. Unlike Donald Sykes, the fiancé who had jilted her almost two years earlier. When her mother's death from consumption on the heels of her father's accidental death, had left her a penniless orphan, she had turned to Donald, fully trusting him to take care of her, only to be let down in the worst possible manner.

For the longest time she had bitterly resented Donald's defection; the more so when she realised he had slyly been courting the daughter of a wealthy businessman while she had been caught up in the heart-rending, unsuccessful struggle to save her mother's life. Until she fell in love with Jason she had been unable to acknowledge, even to herself, that it had been her pride, more than her heart, which Donald had damaged. Now Jason Baker was her whole world.

Fondly, she smiled, filling her eyes with his quite ordinary face, sprinkled with a homely dash of freckles across the bridge of his snub nose.

How much more she preferred the heartfelt honesty and integrity which shone so brightly in Jason's sparkling brown eyes. She'd never be taken in by traitorous good looks again.

The dinner gong rang before she could think what answer to give Jason about the gold, and they descended silently, hand in hand, to the dining room. It was almost impossible to think of anything else, so, each privately mulling over the scheme, they concentrated on their food, returning directly to their room afterwards to continue the discussion out of hearing of their fellow lodgers. It was quite late when they finished thrashing out a mutually acceptable plan and set about getting ready for bed.

*****

Brooding over their plans to spend the following day gathering information on prospecting, and the gold discoveries taking place in the East of the Colony, Eliza sat brushing her hair before bed, soon becoming distracted by the view in the mirror of her husband sitting on the bed behind her.

Absent-mindedly, she admired the way the sun had gilded the tips of Jason's unruly, light brown curls. His skin had acquired a tan from spending every minute he could in the blazing sunshine during the long voyage across the vast Indian Ocean.

He'd fallen into the habit of helping the sailors in their endless tasks, stripped to the waist as they were. She thought he looked as tough and weathered as the sun-bronzed colonial men she'd seen in the town.

Australians, as they called themselves.

Watching him, the sight of those bare, brown arms and sinewy muscles caused her heart to beat faster, and her breath to hitch in her chest. Her eyes slanted sideways to the bed they would soon be sharing, and, a blush staining her cheeks, thought of lying there in her Jason's arms. Her husband's arms.

Catching her watching him, Jason's lips curled into a devilish grin. A grin promising those delights which were still so new to her. Delights she knew she would never tire of. Or have enough of. Jason rose to his feet, coming to stand at her back, trailing his strong, lean hands down her arms. A delicious tension began coiling in the pit of her stomach.

Bending to graze her temple with his lips, Jason took the brush from her fingers and finished brushing out her long, golden ringlets. He loved the sensuous feel of the long tresses sliding through his fingers.

He loved Eliza.

Loved being married to her.

It had been nothing short of a miracle for an orphan from the London slums to win the love of the gently-born girl who had become his wife. Every day Jason silently renewed his vow to improve himself; to become worthy of her.

Right now, eager as he was to have her beneath him in their bed, he couldn't resist the exquisite torment of forcing himself to wait, just a little longer. He dropped a lingering kiss onto the top of her head, the reflected smile it earned him setting a slow burn simmering in his blood.

Eliza sighed with pleasure at the feel of Jason's hands stroking her hair.

Nerve ends tingling, and eager as she was for the satisfaction which would soon be hers, still, she felt too disturbed by the earlier conversation to relax completely and surrender to her husband's ministrations.

"You seem really set on going after this gold, Jason."

She swivelled round on the stool to talk face-to-face, a slight frown creasing her smooth, white forehead.

"Are you so very sure it's the right thing for us to do?"

Irrational fear roiled in her stomach every time she thought about it, but with no valid objection to make, she was not willing to let it cause trouble between the two of them.

She hadn't been married to Jason for long enough to predict his reaction if she set herself steadfastly in opposition to his wishes. However, she really couldn't like the uncertainty of the scheme. There had been far too much uncertainty in her life in recent years, culminating in the huge risk they had taken in emigrating to this strange, new land in search of a better life.

She was very much afraid she lacked her husband's boundless enthusiasm and daring.

Jason looked into the open, honest blue of Eliza's eyes, reading the worry she couldn't hide. Genuine anxiety clouded their depths.

He bit back the easy reassurance which sprang to his lips.

He couldn't lie. Not to the sweetest, most important person in his life. Eliza deserved nothing less than the truth from him. He wasn't on his own any more, making decisions which only affected himself.

He had to think of both of them now.

Love for Eliza had filled the emptiness which had lain for so many years at the centre of his being, yet marriage carried heavy responsibilities he was still coming to terms with.

An unfamiliar pensiveness wiped the smile from his face.

"No," he finally said, so softly Eliza barely heard the word. Voice firming, he resolutely continued.

"No, Eliza darlin, I'm not at all sure and certain it's the right thing. What I am sure of is; if I turn my back on this once-in-a-lifetime opportunity, I'll always regret not givin' it a try."

And resent me for holding you back?

In the silence of her mind Eliza asked the unspoken rider.

A nebulous dread darkened her spirits.

Her Scottish grandmother had claimed to have 'the sight', and once or twice she herself had thought she might have had true premonitions.

Premonitions of disaster, such as the terrible fear which had assailed her one morning while watching her father leave for work. Tempted to call him back, she later wished she had, since that had been the last time she had seen him alive.

This feeling tonight didn't have the same sense of urgency, so maybe it was no more than natural trepidation engendered by the unknown. She prayed it was no more.

Forcing a shaky smile to lips suddenly turned cold and unresponsive, she nodded.

Jason leaned down, his lips claiming hers in the tenderest of kisses.

"I want to give you a good life, wiv all the comforts you deserve, Eliza me darlin'" he told her.

"You and the children we'll be havin', God willin'; and this is a heaven-sent opportunity. It'll be hard work for sure, but it takes more'n hard work to scare me."

He could still read an uncertainty she struggled to hide from him.

"I can see you have reservations, though, Love. If you're dead set against it, I'll give up the idea right this minute and we'll say no more about it. Your happiness is more important than a dream of riches."

Jason pressed his lips to hers once more, in a kiss which felt to Eliza like a solemn promise. Her heart melted, and she kissed him back, her tongue slipping between his parted lips to stroke the inside of his mouth in blatant invitation. To think this good man loved her so much he'd give up his dreams for her, just because she was a silly little scaredy-cat, afraid of taking a risk.

I can't ask it of him. Won't. Eliza reached deep for the courage to abide by her decision. *Not when he's doing it for me as much as himself.* She swallowed, forcing her fears into a tiny corner of her mind.

Instead of trampling on Jason's dreams, she would wholeheartedly do everything within her power to help her man achieve success. A success worked for and shared by them both.

"It's alright, Jason darling," she murmured. "I'm just being silly, letting a woman's foolish fears stand in our way. Let's go dig some gold. Tomorrow. I have other plans for tonight."

*****

Much later that same night, Eliza lay awake, her husband sleeping in her arms. She stroked his curls back from his forehead, careful not to wake him.

The day she met Jason Baker had been the luckiest day of her life.

Everything changed for Eliza that Sunday morning when she had stumbled on the rough steps outside her church; literally falling into Jason Baker's strong arms when he stepped forward to catch her. She had noticed him slipping into a pew in the back of the small church, several weeks in a row, however this was the first time they had met. In later weeks, as she had come to know him for the honest, stalwart young man he was, she had come to think he had been Heaven-sent.

When he rescued her from falling, her heart had beaten faster at the intimate feel of his arms supporting her against his chest, but she had persuaded herself it was the shock of her near accident, not the man.

When he fell into step beside her, chatting as he escorted her back to the Widow Jenkins' house where she rented a room, it had felt as if the sun shone brightly, even though the weather was dull and gusty, with rain threatening.

All through summer they had walked out together, Sunday becoming the highlight of Eliza's week. Not because it was God's day, but because Sunday was the day she saw Jason Baker.

One Sunday afternoon as they followed the tow path beside the river, he told her of a lecture he planned to attend in the church hall on the following Wednesday evening.

A lecture by a friend of the Vicar about a faraway corner of the Empire called Western Australia. A land abounding in strange animals called kangaroos, and flocks of improbably coloured wild parakeets.

"You oughta come wiv me, Lizzie. There's going to be tea and biscuits at the end, and we can ask questions, too. It'll be fun."

Eliza hadn't cared tuppence about the lecture, but since it meant extra hours in Jason's company, she agreed immediately.

That night marked a change in Jason. Eliza noticed he became purposeful, talking about the future, and how he wanted to improve himself. There were frequent references to Western Australia and the abundant opportunities it offered a man willing to work hard to improve himself. Opportunities lacking in England.

The day he told her he had decided to emigrate, she had wept in his arms, fearing she would never see him again. She had only just found him, and she was about to lose him forever.

That was the day she realised she loved Jason Baker with a woman's love.

"Dearest Eliza," he had said, drying his cheeks with his handkerchief, "Don't cry. I didn't mean ta make yer cry. Listen. Hear me out, will yer? Please?"

Sitting beside her on the park bench overlooking the river, he clasped her hands in his, smiling when she obediently turned her face up to him, valiantly holding back her tears.

"I mean the both of us, Lizzie darlin'. I want yer to come to Western Australia wiv me." He blushed, gulped, and said the sweetest words she had ever heard.

"I love yer, Eliza. I want to marry yer. Please say you will. We can get married and go to seek our fortunes in Western Australia together. How about it Lizzie darlin'?"

Agreeing to marry Jason was the easy part. Agreeing to emigrate half-way around the world took considerably more persuasion, but, love outweighing fear, she had agreed.

Now they were here, and a new adventure loomed, threatening to overturn their carefully laid plans.

Their happiness still had the feel of a fairytale come to life, and Eliza didn't regret marrying Jason. Not for one moment; but, oh, how she hoped he'd settle down when he got this gold-fever out of his system. She didn't really believe they would strike it rich, but she would follow him on one more big adventure, then she wanted a home of their own.

She yearned for a settled life.

For a family.

Continued…….

To get

Home is the Heart

as soon as it's released go to

www.lenawestauthor.com

and make sure that you are signed up for news and new release notices!

About the Author

Born in tropical North Queensland, Lena loves living close to the sea, although she moved frequently during her early years, living everywhere from large cities to isolated farms. Her most recent home has a deck overlooking the sea, which is her favourite room in the house, although, when the local birds come to visit, it is often hard to retreat to the computer and write!

After working as a primary school teacher in both her native Queensland, and later in New South Wales where she met her own romantic hero, she took a very early retirement to travel Australia with him, in a motorhome. This idyllic lifestyle lasted several years, during which she took the first steps towards fulfilling her lifelong ambition to write.

Storytelling came naturally - she had been making up stories for her own entertainment all her life, but it wasn't until she began traveling that she had time to write down some of her favourites. Now a self-published author, *Marrying Alan Morgan*, is the first in a series of rural romances set in the fictional town of Oxley Crossing. She also writes standalone contemporary romances and Australian historical romances.

With an addiction to happily-ever-afters, in both her reading and her own stories, the romance genre was a natural fit, and the variety of places she has lived have all added to the settings in which she brings love to life.

You can find Lena on Facebook at:

https://www.facebook.com/LenaWestAuthor/

or sign up for her newsletter at:

www.lenawestauthor.com

Books by Lena West

Historical Romances

Unto Death

https://www.amazon.com/dp/B07D3MZ1L4

Emily's Baby

Lena West

Home is the Heart (Coming soon)

Standalone Contemporary Romances

Loving Fenella

https://www.amazon.com/dp/B07B3RLS98/

Forgotten (Coming soon)

Contemporary Series

Love in Oxley Crossing Series

Marrying Alan Morgan

https://www.amazon.com/dp/B0774V1L25/

Saving Jonathon Armitage

https://www.amazon.com/dp/B0788GCQJQ

Finding Mr Wright

https://www.amazon.com/dp/B07C98B7PJ

Lena West

Electing Robert Whitman

https://www.amazon.com/dp/B07KWKLJG6

Redeeming Josh Marten

https://www.amazon.com/dp/B07RNHBYG7

The Making of Joey Lambert (Coming soon)

The Wyldeflower Series

(Coming soon)

Connect with Lena!

Be the first to know about it when Lena's next book is released!

Sign up to Lena's newsletter at

www.lenawestauthor.com

www.ingramcontent.com/pod-product-compliance
Lightning Source LLC
Chambersburg PA
CBHW050310010526
44107CB00055B/2181